Before I Knew It, They Were Gone

Before I Knew It, They Were Gone

A Jewish First-Generation American
Woman's Journey through the Darkness

Dana R. Neiger

with Phyllis Amaral

BOOKLOGIX

Alpharetta, GA

ISBN: 978-1-6653-0440-5 - Paperback
ISBN: 978-1-6653-0439-9 - Hardcover
eISBN: 978-1-6653-0441-2 - ePub

Library of Congress Control Number: 2022920798

⊚This paper meets the requirements of ANSI/NISO Z39.48-1992 (Permanence of Paper)

1 1 1 6 2 2

I am eternally grateful to my deceased family. If not for them, my life—this book—could not possibly have come together as it has. I dedicate this book to them.

I dedicate it equally to my son, the young man who is, at the time of this writing, only five years old and clueless about his mommy's experiences. I desperately do not want this young man to grow up mediocre or average in any way. His world is wide open before him, and he is capable of achieving anything he can dream of.

If not for you, Deagan, Mommy wouldn't know what true love is. You are my sole purpose in life, and a challenge—in a good way!— reminding me daily to teach, coach, and mentor kindness, empathy, and compassion. You will be better than those family members you know only through stories and pictures.

And you will be better than me.

*What lies behind you and what lies in front of you,
pales in comparison to what lies inside of you.*

—Ralph Waldo Emerson

CONTENTS

PREFACE

T his book tells my life story thus far. It is profoundly personal and writing it has been incredibly therapeutic. But that's not why I wrote it.

I wrote *Before I Knew It, They Were Gone: A Jewish First-Generation American Woman's Journey through the Darkness* in the hope that sharing my journey with those who have experienced death within their family, or suffered a loss, will touch them deeply enough to realize they are not alone.

I also want the reader to know that there are people in the world, quite possibly already in their life, who can relate to what they are going through, even if the reader is not ready to receive help yet.

While the pain is real, so is the honest hope for an even better quality of life at the end of their suffering, despite what they may be thinking at this moment.

The roots of this book grew from the stories I gathered when I reached out to friends and family, curating and solidifying the stories I'd heard, been privy to, and experienced personally. As I reconnected with them to confirm what I thought I knew was accurate, memory being what it is, sharing precious moments of fading memories brought them to life again and proved highly cathartic.

Through this process, I learned that I was not the only one who suffered from the loss of my family members. Hearing stories from my brother's friends and their parents about him and our family gave me one of the most intriguing perspectives. Also, learning that all my friends' parents identified me as a hypersexual child at a young age was an eye-opener. Like a giant math equation, everything added up to an identifiable solution. Finally, the lightbulb came on.

I talk a lot about self-sabotage as part of the process I went through, but grief can express itself differently. Some people turn to drugs, alcohol, or other forms of self-harm, some to therapy, and some choose to simply move on in their own way, whatever that may be. I do not judge, and I am not here to tell you what you should or shouldn't do. I can only share what I went through and hope it is helpful.

I felt it was necessary to be completely transparent in describing my experiences and how I eventually found my way through that terrible sense of isolation and abandonment so the reader can relate—so they can know that those deep, dark thoughts they've had, the anger they feel, or giving up and settling for less than the best life has to offer, isn't unique to them alone.

In this world of nearly eight billion people, I am sure there must be others who have lost their entire immediate family as I did, but I have not met them. I lost my mother and father to cancer exactly one year apart—to the day. Then I lost my brother, my only sibling, out of the blue. All during my twenties, a time when I should have had access to my parents as I graduated from pseudo-adulthood in college to real-world adulting.

Basic, simple tasks, like how to grocery shop appropriately, pay bills, buy a home, date—all these things were beyond my ability in my twenties due to my upbringing. Everything was pretty much taken care of for me. Forget any advice and support around marrying, having a child, building a home and a new life; I was on my own.

Yes, I came from a life of privilege, but loss and suffering transcend all barriers: cultural, economic, generational, language, education, every single one, because loss is part of the human experience. And money cannot replace the people you love and expect will always be there.

I only have my own story of suffering to tell, and I am acutely aware that mine may pale in an objective comparison with many others. Yet, again, it is *my* story, just as you have your story, and those are the only ones of which we have intimate knowledge and can shake us to the core and change the course of our lives.

My story is also about the process of grieving and how critical it is to express it and find support. It's about how leaning in on others can be a good and a bad thing. Timing is crucial, as is the ability to share with someone safely. I've included a resources section at the end of this book, intended to get you started should you want to seek help.

Although we live most of our lives in denial, I believe it is important to acknowledge that death is an inevitable part of life. Death and experiences around loss can leave us feeling very fragile, lonely, and misunderstood. And, perhaps because we can never be truly prepared for it, the devastation, grief, and sense of desperation that so often accompanies the loss of our loved ones can overwhelm us, propelling us into an unhealthy downward spiral.

Yet, another truth is that trauma does not have to hold us back forever. It does not have to become a permanent crutch or a chip on one's shoulder.

Our trials and struggles can also be the source of overcoming strength, tenacity, drive, positivity, and other well-earned and life-affirming qualities!

In hindsight (which always makes us wise), I'd also like to point out the unspoken, yet all-pervasive expectations we grow up with that shout at us that we must achieve certain life goals according to a certain timeline. We have all felt the pressure. But—according to whose timeline? Who gets to set it? And does that make it the *right* timing for everyone?

This is why I live my life on a minimal judgment basis. In a perfect world, no one would judge another person for anything; yet we all do it. Human nature is fascinating and ever-changing. So I'm just here with everyone else trying to live my life too, and maybe, hopefully, offer some helpful, supportive thoughts along the way.

1

The Daughter of French Jewish Immigrants

Many an immigrant story begins in poverty and develops into a highly commendable rags-to-riches theme. Mine does not. In fact, my story begins with wealth and privilege.

I am a first-generation American Jewish woman born of affluent French Jewish immigrants. My father, David, emigrated to the United States several years before my mother, Debi, came over, and it was over a decade before they would eventually meet.

I know very little about their young lives in France or about their parents. I wish I knew more, but Mom and Dad didn't share much. Their reluctance to share personal information is something I came to think of as an "immigrant thing." Growing up, it was just the way things were.

Here's what I do know:

My grandparents on my mother's side, whom I would describe as privileged elitists, followed my mother to this country after she got settled. Her father, my grandfather, Bernie, owned a couple of businesses, one of which was a women's wear store in Chicago (that explains all the stylish outfits I remember Grandma Dorothy always wore!). Later, my uncle David and his wife, Pam, took over the store and eventually sold it.

Grandma Dorothy and Grandpa Bernie traveled a lot during retirement. They worked hard and were very successful, so now they set out to enjoy the final chapter of their lives. The rest of my family thought she was very judgmental; that's not how I remember her, but it would go with an elitist mindset.

I know a little more about my father's side of the family and called that set of grandparents by the traditional Yiddish vernacular: Bobe (pronounced *bub-bee*) was my grandmother, and Zeyde (pronounced *zay*-dee), my grandfather. They were Holocaust survivors and met after the liberation, having lost their spouses in Auschwitz. They seemed very serious to me as a child, and since they passed before I was ten years old, I never really got to know them.

Dad had two sisters, Teddy and Roseline. Aunt Teddy was the oldest sibling and a half-sister, as her father was Bobe's first husband. Teddy was twenty years older than Roseline; my father was seven years older than Roseline. Aunt Teddy married my uncle Joe, left France, and moved to Toronto many years before the rest of the family. Aunt Roseline, the youngest and, now, only surviving sibling, was five years old when she came over with Dad and their parents.

Aunt Roseline once told me a hilarious story of sibling rivalry back in their apartment, which was designed with a courtyard in the middle of the building. (This apartment was in Poland, before Roseline was born.) Roseline explained that one day, her mother, my bobe, said to stay here and be good, "I'm just going to the neighbors for a quick visit." So, Bobe headed over to the neighbor who had an apartment across the courtyard from their own. Next thing she knew, she happened to look out the neighbor's window, across the courtyard to her apartment window where Aunt Teddy was holding my father out the window, shaking and threatening to drop him! I never asked him about it but thank goodness my grandmother came in when she did, or our family story would have taken a dramatic turn from the start!

International and Religious Culture—Cuisine

Because of my family's international and religious origins, I grew up hearing French, Polish, Yiddish, and English spoken among our extended relatives. Far from being a confusing babble, it lent a lovely, harmonious, musical background to our family get-togethers. I loved it, and I also learned to love all aspects of Judaism, all of which is an integral part of who I am today.

My parents raised my brother and me as Conservative Jews, and we faithfully celebrated all the Jewish holy days. We always hosted for Chanukah and Passover—and oh my goodness, the sensory delights they ushered in! I can still smell the fragrant aroma of latkes sizzling in oil for Chanukah and the gefilte fish from my dad's side of the family.

I am next in line to inherit that recipe, by the way—orally, not written, in keeping with tradition. I can still hear chunks of celery and carrots plopping into an enormous pot of water with chicken carcasses that would turn out the best homemade chicken stock ever. And no way can I forget homemade horseradish on Passover that would fry the hairs in your nose!

There were so many wonderfully tantalizing smells, sounds, and family memories surrounding those celebrations. Food that nourished far more than the body, and all of it contributed to a rich, cultural diversity that I fully embraced then and now.

A Slow Start to a Rocket Romance

David, my father, set out for America when he was seventeen to continue his studies here. He entered through New York and stayed to attend the University of Rochester for his undergraduate work. He continued his private school education at Columbia University and landed a job soon after graduating, teaching seventeenth-century French literature at Washington University in St. Louis.

That's where he and my mother, Debi, met. He was the professor, and she, a sophomore—a student in his class. There was a nine-year age difference between them. I don't know if the age difference had anything to do with it, but they tried dating, and it didn't click right away.

My mother majored in Spanish, so now, with no beau to hold her here, she spent her junior year in Spain. While there, she nearly married a Spaniard, so my grandmother had to travel to Spain and retrieve her. Dorothy wanted her youngest daughter to marry a Jewish man, not a Catholic, and create Jewish babies since there are so few of us in the world. Of course, Grandma Dorothy is my source for that information so it's a little sketchy.

Once back at Wash U, my parents started dating seriously, and in true whirlwind-romance style, they were engaged in just six weeks. Then, as soon as Mom graduated, they got married and went to Israel for their honeymoon.

Hijacked!

My Bobe was living in France and had flown to Israel for a cousin's wedding. She had brought wedding gifts for my parents and my cousins, beautiful Judaica—gold and silver candlestick holders, wine glasses, and so on.

She was now on her way back to France. The year was 1976, the date was June 27, and the flight was Air France 139. The plane was en route from Tel Aviv to Paris, with a scheduled stop in Athens, Greece and none of the passengers had any idea what was about to happen.

After leaving Athens, four hijackers stormed the cockpit and took it over at gunpoint. The hijackers, two Palestinian men and two Germans (a man and a woman), were officially aligned with the Popular Front for the Liberation of Palestine-External Operations (PFLP-EO), an integral part of the Palestine Liberation Organization (PLO) terrorist group.

They forced the pilot to land the plane in Entebbe, Uganda, where they were joined by six more PLFP operatives. Bobe was held captive with the other hostages for three terrifying, interminable days and nights before they released her, traumatized, along with some other French citizens. The terrorists had tried to ascertain their captive's ethnoreligious identities, holding Israelis and Jews longer. Bobe's last name was Neiger, French for "to snow," which at least partly explained her release.

Afterward, everyone remembered Brigitte Kuhlmann, the German woman, for her cruelty and fury throughout the entire ordeal. My Bobe was a Holocaust survivor and with their captors' obvious hatred of Jews, I can only imagine what was going through her mind. In the end, almost all the hostages were rescued.

Back at the Ranch

After their honeymoon, and making sure Bobe was okay, my parents returned to St. Louis, where they set up their new home. Not that they had much choice, because her parents wouldn't let them move any farther away. Mom and Dad, however, were ready to begin their life adventures together as their own family unit.

And that's precisely what they did. My father wanted to attend law school next, so he applied to three law schools: the University of Toronto, Boston University, and UCLA in Los Angeles. Both Toronto and Boston U accepted him. Toronto was out because it was too close to St. Louis and their respective families, so Boston it was.

As the story goes, they packed the moving truck the night before and started for Boston. No sooner had they taken off when my father got the news that UCLA Law School had moved him up and off the waitlist and officially accepted him.

They turned that truck around 180 degrees and headed west, as far away from both of their families as they could, toward their new life together.

Los Angeles, here we come!

In Los Angeles, everyone is a star.

—Denzel Washington

✶ 2 ✶

Growing Up in West LA

Dad attended UCLA School of Law while my mother worked at a local auto club for a while. At some point, things weren't going great between them, so I think she got pregnant hoping it would make things better. Of course, we all know how well that works. Regardless, I was born in May 1980, and my brother was born four years later in April—to keep me company and out of her hair. Seriously, that was her plan.

I have some cherished memories of a happy childhood growing up in West Los Angeles, which I still consider home, by the way. We were privileged people living among other privileged people, but it was just normal life for me. Besides, it didn't prevent us from seeing and caring about all people and issues of injustice.

A local litigation firm recruited Dad when he graduated with his law degree. He stayed there for three years until a Japanese multinational electronics and electrical equipment manufacturing company recruited him as corporate in-house general counsel, and he made the long daily commute from LA to Orange County.

Having worked in legal recruiting myself, I can attest to the fact that my father must have worked his butt off to get out of the typical churn-and-burn life of a billable-hours attorney and into an in-house attorney position with regular office hours. It's rare for it to happen so quickly, especially at such a young age.

When my parents moved to LA, they bought a standard, original, 1940s Beverly Hills house right away. Like many homes in West LA, it sat on a small lot, making backyard space scarce. The house was yellow with a little, dark wooden deck in the back with three precarious steps leading down to the small grassy area that was our backyard. Bright, fuchsia-colored bougainvillea ran rampant through the property, along with a single lemon tree that provided the occasional lemon for Mom to pick.

Two of my earliest memories are carefree and comforting. The first is a very young me padding barefoot through the house, pulling a small wooden doggie on wheels that barked as it rolled along. It probably annoyed the hell out of everyone, but at that age, who cares? I loved it, and it accompanied me everywhere.

I also remember running down the hall and jumping into bed with my parents to snuggle, perfectly safe, content, and with the inarticulate but certain knowledge that all was well in my small, young world.

Trapped!

I was born in May 1980 and my brother, Stephen, was born in 1984. I must have been four or five years old at the time. My parents were in the garage with its original, clunky door, a heavy wooden thing with a big, old, rusty spring attached. Well, the spring snapped, and the door slammed down hard, trapping Mom and Dad inside. They could not get it to budge, no matter how hard they tried. And they tried hard because baby Stephen was all alone in the house. In his crib, but still alone, making it a perfect time for young parents to panic.

I was on the other side of the garage door, so my parents called to me and gave me careful instructions about going across the street to ask our neighbors, the Walkers, for help.

"Look both ways, Dana!" they repeated over and over.

My young mind processed the directive, and I set off to complete the mission. I stopped at the side of the road, looked both ways, then continued across the street to our neighbor's house and knocked on their front door. The Walkers had two daughters, Sharon and Katie, and were friends with my parents, so they knew who I was, but it surprised them to see me there by myself. There was a birthday party going on, so they kindly invited me in and offered me some birthday cake. *Umm, yes, please!*

With my focus abruptly shifted and the original mission forgotten, my dopamine centers already firing away in anticipation, I headed over for my slice of birthday cake. It wasn't until I had almost finished it that I remembered to announce, "Mommy and Daddy are stuck in the garage and they need help." Katie and her dad ran over immediately to check on them and Stephen. Then they got a few strong neighbors to pry the door open enough for my parents to crawl out, thus leaving this story with a happy ending for all.

Over the years, Katie Walker became a dear friend and it is she who told me that story; I confess I don't remember it, but she does because it was her sister's birthday party. Katie was a few years older than me, but we became great friends, and we are still close today. She also recalls that I was a sound sleeper during our subsequent, frequent sleepovers, even sleeping through a few earthquakes. Maybe at some level, it felt like being rocked, I don't know, but it amazed everyone that I never woke up.

The Walkers

I learned manners from the Walkers. As I got older, my parents insisted I call them Mr. and Mrs. Walker instead of addressing them by their first names like many more-liberal people in LA let their children do in the '80s. They also trained me to answer the phone: "Hello, this is Dana. Who's calling, please?" This was because the Walker daughters, Katie and Sharon, answered the phone this way, and my parents loved how it sounded.

Their script was actually, "Hello, this is Katie/Sharon Walker speaking. How can I help you?" Either way, those two girls and their parents made a powerful impression on my parents. Katie and Sharon were like big sisters growing up, and I tutored with Sharon through elementary and middle school. She was key in helping me with math deficiencies mainly, but also in reading comprehension.

Mr. and Mrs. Walker still live in the same house today and are still two of the kindest, most compassionate, and caring people you could ever meet.

The Remodel

Original houses have loads of charm and character, but they also need expensive updating at some point. So, when my dad made it big some years later, they remodeled our home.

The builders gutted the house, so we had to move out. My mother was the project manager on the remodel since my father had "more important things to do." But they both came back frequently to inspect the progress. I remember looking up where the roof used to be and seeing the stars one evening. It felt exciting . . . and scary at the same time. I didn't have words for it then, but somehow, I knew that my home wasn't a safe haven anymore and wouldn't be until the walls, ceilings, and roof were back in place.

For some reason unclear to me now, I remember the general contractor's name was Arpad, he wore blue jeans, and he was very nice. Anyway, my mother was always very creative, so after the contractors had pretty much finished the remodel, she asked Arpad to bring over all the leftover tiles. Any color, the more the merrier. She had an idea for the downstairs bathroom.

So, he brought over boxes and boxes of discontinued, leftover, half-broken, four-by-five tiles in the brightest and most hilariously obscene colors of raspberry, fuchsia, peach, and lime green you can imagine. Perfect!

Mom figured out the pattern she wanted and showed the contractors exactly how she wanted them to go, explaining everything in fluent Spanish. So, they laid those dramatic and *bright* tiles halfway up the bathroom walls and all the way up to the ceiling in the shower and bath area. And so was born what we lovingly dubbed our Sunglasses Bathroom.

To complete the project, my aunt Karin, one of Dad's friends from law school, brought over the latest *People* magazines with hotties on the cover to grace the lovely new magazine holder in the bathroom. Clearly, reading material was a big thing in our circle.

A project that size takes ages, but we had a brand-new house and lots more room when it was finally done. My mom celebrated with a housewarming party and sent out invitations she'd made in the shape of a tiny version of our new home.

She ended up redoing nearly everything in the landscape too. She had a rock garden put in and planted strawberries, poppies, and snapdragons. Strawberries—I didn't understand that they started out green, turned yellow-y white, and finally red before I could eat them. Or how long to let them grow before the birds and bugs got to them first. Mom explained they got hungry too, and it was okay to let them eat. I have had the same conversation in our strawberry patch with our son when the dogs snuggle in and eat them—at any stage!

Mom also showed me how to make poppies and snapdragons "talk" by squeezing them a certain way. As a young girl, that was enchanting to me. Finally, only the bougainvillea remained from the original landscape; that same lovely, hot-pink vine now graced the new fence separating our driveway and the garage area.

Our house became the biggest house on the block; it's the second biggest now. I am still friends with some of the neighbors, and on one of my visits back as an adult, I got to go through our house again. That brought back so many memories, even with the changes they'd made to it.

The new owners—a movie producer and his soap-actress wife—had lived there briefly before moving back to New York after losing her parents. When they decided to sell it, she did me the honor of offering it to me first for a mere $2 million. I politely declined.

Famous Neighbors

Living in Beverly Hills, it isn't surprising that we had some famous neighbors. I remember one man always walking the biggest dog I had ever seen in my life. It was a giant English mastiff named Benjamin, and it turned out the man was the owner of one of the two real "Beasts" used in some scenes in the 1990s movie series *The Sandlot*. That dog was a real sweetheart.

My dad had some famous clients, and he knew other celebrities either directly or through his law school friends. Celebrity neighbors whose names you would recognize immediately but like to sue anyone who even mentions them, so . . . not mentioning them. Although one "real" famous family lived in the neighborhood then, whose last name begins with a "K" . . . Just saying.

Falling for Dennis Quaid

I was in line with my aunt Karin at the Century City movie theater in LA. In the late '80s, it was *the* group of theaters to go to, and I was super excited just to be seeing a movie with her. I was also being my usual fidgety eight-year-old self.

Aunt Karin and I were holding hands and doing that arm swing game, back and forth. I took it too far, lost my balance, and stumbled backward into someone. I recovered my footing and Aunt Karin calmly put her hand on my shoulder. I looked up at her as she whispered, "Be still, and I'll tell you who that is behind you." So, I was perfectly still while she told me, cool as a cucumber, that I had just fallen into Dennis Quaid.

Even at that young age, I knew who the ever-so-handsome Dennis Quaid was. I'd seen the *Jaws* movies and loved them all. I was learning to surf, and sharks, for some reason, intrigued me.

Past tense, to be sure. So, we quietly kept our place in line in front of Dennis Quaid and Meg Ryan, his wife at the time.

We also had random celebrities drop in on us at home. My husband was looking through an old photo album the other day and spotted Jeff Goldblum in a picture with baby Stephen at his bris. The bris, or Brit Milah, is a Jewish ceremony on the eighth day of a baby boy's life and involves circumcision and giving them their name. I'm not sure how that came about, but clearly, it did.

Also, as part of the multinational electronics and electrical equipment manufacturing company's general counsel team and their sponsorship of the UCLA basketball team, Dad worked on contracts for many of the players here and overseas and for the UCLA head coach. With sports now such an integral part of our daily lives, it isn't surprising that I became a sports fan early on.

All I really need to know I learned in kindergarten.

—Robert Fulghum

∗ **3** ∗

Toddling off to the Games

Our son, Deagan, started kindergarten this year, which brought back memories of my preschool days.

My mother worked in the University Park area of Los Angeles, close to USC (University of Southern California) then, so my parents sent me to a nearby preschool. By now, they were close friends with the Walkers, long-time employees at USC and huge USC football fans.

A Young Fan

My parents often went to the games with the Walkers. Apparently, my father thought it would be hilarious to dress me in T-shirts from rival teams when they dropped me off at childcare on the way. So there I was, innocently offering some serious conflict opportunities, wearing Notre Dame and Michigan T-shirts—teams that are still USC's biggest rivals to this day.

I'm sure the childcare staff, and probably quite a few of the parents, got some laughs out of it. So, yeah, I didn't have many friends back then. But seriously, I was a tiny Trojan from a very early age. This is where my love for USC sports began, and, in fact, I consider myself a USC alumnus. I figure there aren't many people who can trace their collegiate sports roots that far back, right?

I've mentioned the Walkers a few times now, and Katie

Walker in particular. Over the years, she became more like a sister to me. She still lives in LA, but we stay in touch, especially during football season. Katie is one of the few women I know who speaks the language of football and knows the stats even better than me. Now that's saying something!

Handle with Kid Gloves

I also made my foray into the world of baseball at an early age. My USC campus preschool held an annual Parents Day event. They selected a group of us to welcome the parents, and we were supposed to hold up a banner while singing "Take Me Out to the Ballgame" along with the team. Cute, right?

My dad gave me my very own, brand-new, leather baseball glove for the occasion. In case you don't know, there's a special ritual that goes with a new leather glove. You put your ball in the middle of the glove, throw some oil on it, wrap the glove with rubber bands around everything, and let it sit as it soaks in the oil. They call this process "manhandling the glove," and it was all very special and exciting to me.

However, this particular Parents Day event also commemorates the only time I remember freezing with stage fright. I practiced singing with the team but completely froze when the real thing happened. I mean, I couldn't move or speak, much less sing, so I didn't get to be part of the event, something I still regret.

To the best of my recollection, nothing like that has ever happened to me since. I make sure I am perfectly prepared for all presentations!

*A daughter needs a dad to be the standard
against which she will judge all men.*

—Gregory E. Lang

* **4** *

A Scholar and a Lawyer

My father was a brilliant man. He was all about education and the unlimited doors he believed knowledge and good grades could open for you in life. However, he was an overachiever and very proud of his multiple degrees in law and academia. Dad was also an elitist who had no patience with anyone who couldn't keep up with him. Unfortunately, that included most people. Anyone who wasn't as bright as him was simply not worth his time, and his priorities were the ones that mattered.

Stand There and Take It

My father chose his words carefully, so he was always telling me, "Don't be an airhead, Dana—think before you speak!" According to his standards, naturally, I got called "airhead" a lot. He had a habit of using his well-chosen words in a way that commanded respect and expected obedience. He demanded it of my mother and me too. Some of it made me tough, built a protective shell around me when I needed one, and helped me excel in sports. It also kept me isolated when I most needed to let others in.

He required serious effort in my studies and accepted nothing less than As and 100s. When that didn't happen, we'd do a major debriefing about *why* I hadn't aced the test or quiz, and then we'd go through it again to make *sure* I understood what I'd gotten wrong.

He used the term "put out" to describe expending energy in my studies, but as I got older and understood the term in its sexual connotation, I grew to despise it. I would beg him to adjust his wording since I felt it was demeaning and sexist, but he would laugh like a crazed person and tell me *no, just deal with it.* Still figuring that one out.

I remember standing nose to nose with him, literally, him shouting in my face without allowing me to respond in any way. This didn't happen every day, but when it did, I had to stand there and silently, impassively, take it. During these sessions, he'd be all in my face. His eyebrows would start twitching, but it was his eyes I remember most. They would open monstrously, and the whites of his eyes became enormous. I hated it. Then, when that day's yelling session was over, he'd say, "Good. Now let's see if we can improve on the time you can take it tomorrow."

Just Talk to Me

Some people "disappear" during trauma as a survival mechanism. They mentally and emotionally compartmentalize, pushing down the painful reality of the event, whether it's verbal or physical, like rape or any other form of abuse. Me? I was 100 percent dialed in when he was yelling at me because I have perfect aural memory. Anything I hear, if I'm listening and it connects, sticks with me pretty much forever, so I could never let my mind even wander during those times. This is probably why I'm both able and not able to take yelling as an adult.

Between the yelling exercises and his increasing focus on me (more on that later), I grew mentally strong and could get through difficult situations. It also meant that sometimes I lacked sensitivity and could be a bitch. Okay, I can still be a bitch. Friends have said over the years that it's better to be on my good side than elsewhere, and I can't disagree. It has caused me to suffer too, and it's something I continue to work on. Especially my RBF (resting bitch face). I'm still working on that. Just ask my husband.

Fractured Body Image

Body image is also difficult to talk about. I know many women struggle with this for various reasons. My dad was always putting me down for my body shape, and because I didn't understand why, I became hypersensitive about the way I'm built. I continue to deal with that, despite a loving husband who thinks I'm perfect—not arguing with him about that!

Dad always wanted me to cover up, especially my butt. Nothing tight or form-fitting, and no dresses or skirts that could even remotely draw attention to my body. Looking back, I realize it was because I was attractive, with curves in all the right places, and it was his way of trying to protect me.

But instead of protecting me, it gave me a lousy body image and opened the door to a lot of self-shaming. Those long-sleeve flannel shirts that got tied at the bottom for that '90s grunge look? That was me. Lots of bulky sweatshirts too.

To this day, I don't wear skirts or dresses very often, and when I do, they've gotta hit the knee. It has taken me a long time to get this far, to love and accept myself as I am. When I see some people fat-shaming others, I understand it's *their* issue. *They* are insecure, and that is often what insecure people do—tear others down to make them feel better about themselves.

Family Traits

When we were still living in LA, my dad and I would go to a local video chain store and peruse the shelves packed with videos for family movie night. One time, we were heading back to the car with our selections when a homeless man approached us. My father ordered me to get in the car while he went and talked with him. Dad came back shortly and grabbed all the change he

21

could find and gave it to the man. I'd never seen that side of him before, and while it may not seem like a big deal to anyone else, the moment touched me.

At five foot seven, my father was the same height as my mother. As a man, he was a powerhouse in a small package, but in his youth, he got bullied. His father, also about the same height and powerful, compact build, was there when it happened. He grabbed the bully by the back of the collar and pulled him down to his level. I don't know what he said to the guy, but my father had no trouble with him after that.

These two men imparted many of their values and traits to me, including the instinct to protect and stand up for the rights of others. Like the time in college when Melanie, my good friend, standing at only five feet tall, and I, pushing six feet, used to go clubbing together. She "hired" me as her bodyguard and we had a blast, but I still have that instinct. Now I do it in other, further-reaching and longer-lasting ways in my personal life and my business.

I also got a kind of fearlessness from my father. This came in handy in the '90s when we, a Jewish family, moved from big-town, liberal, more socially conscious LA to Gainesville, a small country town in Georgia. We landed less than a mile up the road from a KKK Grand Wizard.

My mother was genuinely concerned, but it didn't bother me at all. I knew I could take care of myself, so it didn't scare me. Doubtless, a part of my confidence also stemmed from the fact that at sixteen, I was already five feet, eleven inches tall, weighed between 130 and 140 pounds, and was in great shape because of all the sports I'd played. Still.

But I'm getting ahead of myself.

I said my dad was a yeller. He also ordered my mother around. A *lot*. He treated her like she was inferior to his superior lawyer abilities, and he would manipulate her with heavy negotiating skills. I didn't know this then, but in later conversations with my aunts Karin and Charlotte, friends of Dad's from law school, it turns out they used to coach Debi on her "negotiations" with Dad. This coaching eventually gave her the confidence to stand up for herself.

She started defending herself so well that my dad phoned both ladies and yelled at them to stop helping Debi! It made him furious. They would both calmly say, "Equal opportunity." They tried to explain that they were just trying to give her some confidence and perspective, but it infuriated him.

I realize now their well-intentioned and extremely helpful interference helped Mom negotiate their marriage as well as she did.

My Father's Office

Part of our West LA home remodel included a new office for my father. He had it painted hunter green and furnished it with a cream-colored leather couch and rich, red mahogany furniture. His desk chair had a wooden back with arms and octopus legs with wheels for rolling around.

It was very much a dark, male office, but the ambiance wasn't all somber. My dad had a mallard-shaped phone whose eyes would light up red and quack when anyone called. Stephen and I loved it, of course. Mom hated it. He also had an answering machine with this message: "Congratulations! You've reached the Ultimate Answering Service, and it has your undivided attention. Please speak your mind at the beep." He thought that was a riot. Mom just rolled her eyes.

One of the room's decorations was a rock paperweight Dad kept on his desk. I had gotten it for him while on a trip when I was nine. A child's gift of love that, of course, didn't go with anything else in his office, but he kept it all the same, right there on his desk.

My father forbade me to go into his office, so, naturally, I snuck in as often as I could. It felt like Dad, and it smelled like Dad. He was a pipe smoker, and when he smoked, the cloud would drift lazily through the air before settling like a blanket and bonding with the walls and furniture. His favorite pipe tobacco was vanilla-scented, which he always hand-stuffed into his pipe. Once in a while, I swear I can still smell that delicious, comforting, vanilla-tobacco scent, and I believe that's him letting me know he is near.

I absolutely *loved* playing Office in there and rolling around on those octopus legs. This is also where I got into mischief on at least one memorable occasion.

Seventh Grade and the Great Diamond Experiment

It was 1993, and I was in the seventh grade, having just transitioned from my last year in elementary school in LA to Palms Middle School, a brilliant magnet school. It was a veritable melting pot of remarkable diversity with kids from various backgrounds, religions, and learning abilities. I kept my core group of mostly Jewish friends, but I also made lots of cool, new ones that turned into long-term friendships. We also had an eclectic bar mitzvah to attend pretty much every weekend that year.

Mr. Lasky was my seventh-grade biology teacher. Hearing the word "biology" still makes me laugh. Even before we moved to Georgia, my mom had an inside joke about it. My parents would say to each other, "Bah-ahlogy is the sah-ence of lahfe," in their best Southern drawl. It cracked them up every time.

Anyway, to this day, I can remember several things I learned from Mr. Lasky that year, one of which had to do with diamonds. Mr. Lasky taught us how diamonds form and are so sharp and strong they can cut glass. I found this fascinating. And I decided to test it with my own experiment.

My mother had a beautiful set of two-carat diamond earrings, an anniversary gift from my father. I knew where they stored them in Dad's office, so one day I slipped in, grabbed the box with its treasure, and lifted the blinds. As I removed an earring in preparation, I remember thinking, "Let me scratch this down the window and see if it's real." I also remember the shock that immediately followed. "Oh s*it, it's real!"

Somehow, I had the presence of mind to lower the blinds before running away, but I don't remember putting the box away or even if I got into trouble for it.

Mr. Lasky was also the person who helped us realize we had inappropriately named the two desert tortoises my parents bought for Stephen and me. It became clear when we looked at the bottom part of Laverne and Shirley's shells as he had taught us. Oops, they're both males! We immediately renamed them Siskel and Ebert.

The Youngest at Passover

I was about four years old one Passover, before Stephen was born, making me the youngest member of the family. It's a tradition in Jewish culture that the youngest family member asks the four questions that are asked at every Passover. One can do it in Hebrew or English, and Dad decided that nothing less than Hebrew would be good enough.

So he recorded the questions on a big cassette recorder to help me memorize them and showed me how to use the machine. I played that tape over and over and over until I had it right, and when Passover came, my earnest little four-year-old self asked those four questions in perfect Hebrew.

As I write this, my son is getting ready for Passover in the spring of 2022, and I want to let him decide if he wants to do it. I'm not sure it's good to force someone so young to do something they may not be ready for. It needs to be his decision, but I admit to crossing my fingers.

A Father's Dreams for His Son

My dad was ecstatic when Stephen was born. I have a picture

of Dad cradling my infant brother in his arms, along with a baby bat and ball. That picture speaks volumes to me about Dad's hopes and plans for his son in the coming years. But he was terribly disappointed when he realized Stephen had cognitive and learning issues. His dreams died, and that's when he began ignoring my brother and focusing all his attention on me.

I'm pretty sure now that Stephen had ADHD, along with other issues, but back then they didn't recognize or understand it as we do now. It must have been too difficult for my father to deal with, so that left my mother to handle his special needs and ongoing challenges.

The Other Shoe Drops

Many years later, my parents bought me a brand-new car for my sixteenth birthday. Unfortunately, I ran it through a wood fence just two weeks later.

What I recall most about that incident is that my parents didn't get mad at me, at least not right away. I steeled myself, expecting my father to ream me out—but he didn't. Nothing. Then, a week or two later, when I did something *really* irresponsible, like not putting the cap on the toothpaste, he exploded, and I exhaled. *Ah, there it is.*

To describe my mother would be to write about
a hurricane in its perfect power.

—Maya Angelou, *I Know Why the Caged Bird Sings*

5

Dance or Sports?

I adored my mother. No other word comes close to describing how enamored I was with her. She could do no wrong in my eyes, and I wanted not just to be like her, I wanted to *be* her. I constantly craved her attention and would have deliriously consumed all of it but, sadly for me (and luckily for her), it was not to be.

Stephen had a tough time in school with his learning challenges, so Mom spent many hours helping him with his homework, getting him tested, and so on. That took up a lot of her time, which I understood then only as time away from me.

Following in My Mother's Footsteps

As in most families, our relationship became more complicated as I got older, but for the longest time, I was determined to follow in her footsteps. Every step, every turn she took. Even with her hair. She dyed it for as long as I can remember, so, of course, I couldn't wait to grow up and dye mine.

She had long, beautiful hair until she underwent radiation and chemo for the cancer that eventually killed her. It grew back gray and coarse, so I will never know when she would have gone gray naturally. Her natural hair color was a mousy brown, but I only remember her as a blond. And later when she experimented with a variety of colors on the top of her head!

My mother was gorgeous. Everyone told her so, and they always led with that statement when describing her. While I'm sure she was vain in her way, she seemed down-to-earth to me. She had a dancer's body, long and lean, and a natural scent that imparted a sense of comfort and calm. I still smile now, thinking about it.

She loved expensive perfumes, but to me, she smelled the best right after waking up. So I'd sneak in and cuddle next to her inside her bedsheets some mornings before school. I had to sneak in since my father was more restrictive about their private suite. But she'd cuddle with me, and she smelled like warm skin, a bit like sandalwood. Even her morning breath wasn't that bad.

Dressing Up

Mom's creative talents extended to sewing, and she made several of my first Halloween costumes. One was a can-can girl costume that was to die for, another a princess costume that doubled as Queen Esther for the Jewish holiday of Purim.

One of my favorite costumes was Elvira. If that's before your time, Elvira was a very sexy woman who dressed like a vampire and introduced *terrible* monster movies that everyone loved to watch.

For that one, Mom put me in a long black wig, added vampire teeth, did my makeup, and wrapped me in her black wrap dress that reached to the floor on me. And then stuffed the front of it with socks. Hey, I was supposed to look like Elvira, and she was one sexy vampire.

Then I wanted to be a 1950s cheerleader like Mom had been, so she made me a bubble gum–pink poodle skirt from scratch and added her letterman sweater with the letter R on it. I'm guessing the R was for her school. She said to wear the sweater like a cape over the shoulders and carefully instructed me to fasten only the first button.

She made the skirt and poodle from heavy felt fabric, and we borrowed a crinoline from the Walkers, cotillion enthusiasts. White saddle shoes and ankle socks with delicate ruffles on the top, a cute white blouse, and a ponytail completed the '50s look. I loved all the costumes she made for me, and I realize now that she probably had as much fun with them as I did.

Like many little girls, I also loved it when she dressed me up in her grown-up costume jewelry. This memory is rather vague, just bits that may not be completely accurate because I was two years old, but I enjoy picturing it in my mind.

My mother had taken me along with her to Miami to attend a funeral, where we stayed in a friend's guest room. She awoke in the wee hours of the morning and heard me in the attached bathroom. She approached quietly and saw that I had opened her makeup bag and was playing with everything in it. My mother watched me play with her lipsticks, mascara, and various tubes, bottles, and palettes bursting with color. As a result, I was covered, but she told me once, as an adult, that she thought it was adorable even then.

All About Dance

Mom was also a professional dancer. In the mid- to late 1980s, she performed in large dance scenes in several movies. It was exciting for all of us, and I remember watching take after take, never once feeling bored. They were all so glamorous in their '80s-style makeup and costumes! She was also asked to be in an exercise video with the troupe and several of her friends; I think it was called *Ellie's Way*.

For a while, she was involved with a semi-pro women's dance troupe who shared her love of African American dance, Mom's specialty. They rehearsed in various studio locations, and the studios fascinated me. I remember their primary studio in West LA. They had the second floor of a two-story, brown-and-tan, boxy, industrial-looking building. After entering through the front door, you immediately walked up a short flight of stairs to reach the loft.

Big bay windows lined the room, tinted glass stretching floor to ceiling, with a ballet bar running across them at adult waist-level. The tinted windows gave some protection from the light and heat, but even with the air conditioner working overtime, it got hot in the summer. During practice, the AC also did little for the pervasive, mixed odors of everyone's sweat. The air was always damp then, almost musty, but it would have been much worse without the constant airflow.

This studio was my second home, and I loved running around with a fellow ballet student. We basically terrorized the place, running everywhere, into every room. We were a bit wild, but we didn't hurt anything, and it was great fun.

The Dancers

I loved being in the dressing room with the adult dancers, just watching them. They had gorgeous leotards, brightly colored leg warmers, and their makeup was flawless. I remember thinking, as an outsider, that they had the most disgusting feet I'd ever seen. Their feet were extraordinarily rough-looking and *covered* in callouses. However, pedicures weren't for them because their feet *had* to be tough. Those callouses protected them so they could perform their strenuous, rhythmic, exquisite moves.

Behind the scenes or offstage, they were regular people, mostly professionals in other areas of life. Some were doctors, lawyers, nurses, insurance brokers, and homemakers. They studied massage techniques and gave each other frequent massages to relax their overworked muscles; and I remember all the popping sounds as they cracked each other's backs.

But my best memories around dance are all about the gorgeous costumes in shades of fuchsia, teal, tan, and hot pink. And every dancer wore a bandana for their long hair, very '80s. Mom always wore a navy blue or red bandana wrapped around her forehead to catch the sweat. (I still have her red one.) I loved it all so much that even when I was ready to quit dance, I was half tempted to stay just for the costumes and the incredible camaraderie they shared.

Kurt Russell, Gentleman

There were dance classes for the children too, and this studio attracted a lot of celebrities. Mom always gushed over how Kate Hudson and I were in a few classes together. A story she told even more often was the time Kate's dad, Kurt Russell, opened the door to the studio for her and held it open as she walked through.

I enjoyed hearing these stories because I didn't know who Kate or her dad was back then. She was just a nice girl in my ballet class that we all called Katie, and she and I had a blast running around the studio. Yes, that was my running companion! She was a year older than me, and we lost touch soon after, but I remember those times fondly and still think of her as Katie.

Decision Made!

I took dance lessons until I was nine years old. At my mother's insistence, I started with the classics, ballet and tap. There was more "style" within ballet and tap back then, and I spent some decent years at it. However, I knew that my body type was different from most dancers'. While I'd noticed a few curvier exceptions in my mother's group, most dancers were skinny and lean, while back then I was skinny and muscular all over. I could tell dancers weren't *supposed* to look like me, and I knew I wouldn't grow up to look like them. But that was only part of it.

Dad also helped with my decision to leave dance. He made me stay with it until I was nine and then gave me an ultimatum: dance or sports. He wanted me to be serious about sports, but now I understand that was too much pressure for a nine-year-old. Still, I loved sports and would have eventually gravitated in that direction anyway. Looking back, I don't think it disappointed Mom when I quit. At least she didn't show it to me, and maybe she and Dad had talked it over.

Picking Up on Independence

As I got older and my mother went back to work in the insurance industry, still dancing off-hours, I wanted all of that too. The West LA waxings, the nails, the clothes—and the independence. Watching her as closely as I always was, I picked up on my mother's non-verbal cues, like giving dad the side-eye, those kinds of things. I knew Dad's treatment of her didn't always go over very well.

So, while she never openly counseled me on it, at some point I decided I didn't need a man to tell me what to do, how to dress, or how to be intellectually stimulating. I knew I had everything I needed to make my way in life even then. After all, I had already learned how to manipulate others into doing my chores for me, which I now see as the beginning of my "relationship-management skills." And while Mom didn't exactly support what I was doing, she would say in an aside to me, "Nice skills."

Can We Please Talk about Sex?

Years later, after we'd moved to Georgia, one thing I really wanted to bond with my mother about was sex. Because, once we lived in the Bible Belt of the South, there was no one I could talk to about it. When I tried to bring it up, she would look at me like I was crazy and tell me it was inappropriate for us to discuss that. Her view was that they were my parents, not my friends. Dad's philosophy on the subject was, "Don't ask, don't tell."

The only "conversation" I recall having with either of them on that subject was when I was four years old. My little brother had just been born, and I asked my parents where babies came from. They went into the whole "Mommy and Daddy love each other" thing, rambling on for a few minutes until I broke in with, "So you and Daddy had sex twice?" They looked at each other and just said, "Yup." That was as far as I ever got.

Interestingly, many years later, my friend Katie (Walker) told me she and my Mom had been close enough to share those kinds of intimate conversations. This was when Katie was going through some serious challenges in her marriage. So, while I'm honestly happy for Katie, I'm also a little sad that I never got to confide in my mom.

Winning isn't everything; it's the only thing.
If you can shrug off a loss, you can never be a winner.

—Vince Lombardi

* **6** *

All about Sports

There is a focus and determination-to-win mentality that's a Vince Lombardi thing. He was and is an inspiration to millions of athletes. When I finally made the switch from playing sports to professional coaching, I quoted him to my girls.

I have fond memories of most sports-related things. Although there was that one time my dad insisted I make my first real, grown-up decision involving a sports event. I hadn't had my bat mitzvah yet, so I must have been around ten years old. Being Jewish, religion was always important to my family. The choice was between a religious retreat and a soccer tournament, and I knew I had to choose the religious thing. So that's what I did, but I was super pissy about it.

Sports were many things to me over the years. They helped me focus, grow stronger physically and mentally, and they also provided an outlet. I entered the sports world at the tender age of three and stayed until injuries forced me to quit playing and switch to professional coaching. I worked hard at it and excelled at most sports, so that helped to hold my interest. But more importantly, they provided opportunities to try to bond with my father. As much as I sought my independence, I was always looking for his approval and praise.

My dad was an assistant coach for some of my earlier recreation-league soccer teams, for which I played goalie. As I got a little older, however, I think he realized it wasn't a good idea, or maybe he just didn't have time. Whatever the reason, I was glad when he stopped coaching because he was meaner as a coach. Besides, when he was just a spectator, I could show off for him.

Then Dad became a center-line referee for some boys' soccer teams. He was a legit referee too. I think he started doing it for the exercise, but it turned out he enjoyed it. Staff was often short of line refs for center field, so I filled in for him sometimes. By middle school, I was lining for him frequently on the weekends, fitting it in around my own games, and things got a little confusing. Worst of all, the boys he refereed for were all friends of mine from school, so I'd always hear about the errors he'd called that they felt were unfair.

After every one of my games, there was a post-mortem with Dad. It was a depressing review on bad days, and on good days—well, not really good, but not so bad. He'd go over what I did wrong and how I could have done better, always striving for perfection. And, of course, as a goalie in soccer, you're the last line of defense. You've *got* to know what you're doing to not let that ball get past you.

Team vs. Individual Sports

Team sports were much more to my liking than individual ones like tennis and skiing. I learned very early on that individual strengths did not transfer well to single sports. *Mental quicksand* describes it nicely. Just as physical quicksand responds to pressure and pulls you down, so does mental quicksand. When things start going wrong in a game, negative thoughts follow, and soon the momentum builds. Before you know it, you can't dig yourself out of the hole you've just dug for yourself, and you keep making mistakes. It's a very lonely place to be.

So, I thrived in my sports teams. I loved the team culture and the buzz, plus they brought out the natural leader in me. They also had a calming influence that individual sports did not, because there, it was so easy to be hard on myself. I took on my father's critical mentality, and those thoughts messed with my head. I was still responsible for my metrics and outcomes in team sports, but there was a big difference. And I played a lot of both kinds over the years, like swimming, skiing, tennis, softball, soccer, and basketball.

Soccer was my favorite, hands-down. It was also the first sport I ever played, so that may have been a factor, but I also loved halftime in soccer. It meant water and orange slices—the *best* snack ever. We all had orangey, smiley faces before giving them up to revel in refreshing bursts of sweet juice in every bite. Oh yeah.

Soccer is boring to many people, but it becomes so much more entertaining when you understand the strategies, plays, and stats. Strategy in any sport, like seeing space and passing lanes, but especially in soccer and basketball—takes you to a whole new level of enjoyment.

Halftime at the Rose Bowl

I loved playing in the rec league American Youth Soccer Organization (AYSO) for West LA with all my friends. I did that for about five years, from four to nine years old. The goal in the league was making it through to the playoffs, which our team often did. The playoffs were a chance to play the best teams around the greater metro Los Angeles area.

Best of all, back then the city champions got to play at the Rose Bowl halftime every year—and I got to participate one year. The LA AYSO comprised two divisions, and the winning teams got to play each other for about twenty minutes during halftime. It was short and fun, but it was also serious for us.

I also played in the Turkey Tournament at UCLA every Thanksgiving. Sometimes I got recruited to a different city team if my home team didn't make it. Maybe that wasn't as big a deal as getting to play at the Rose Bowl Stadium, but it was my first experience of feeling important and valued, and it felt wonderful.

In 2018, my husband and I flew to LA to watch his favorite college football team, the UGA (University of Georgia) Bulldogs, play at the Rose Bowl Stadium, and we watched them win. Sitting there in that ninety thousand–plus capacity seating stadium, in my USC T-shirt, I looked around, remembering the time I had played there so long ago. It was the largest environment I'd ever played in, and even though the game was super short, to this day, I think of that amazing experience every time I watch a game being played there.

The Game

And yet, there was an even greater, more momentous event early on in my life that involved soccer.

I was about seven, playing goalkeeper for the first time, and I was ready. I saw the ball come flying toward the left corner of the goal, my right side, and I dove in to block it. When I stood up, that precious, dirty, white ball cradled in my arms, I heard my father yell, "Beautiful!" He was clapping like mad, shouting wonderful things to me.

Like a scene in a movie, everything else faded away. All I saw or heard was my father as I processed the fact that I had pleased him, along with the dawning realization that he was proud of me. I wanted to bathe in the warmth of that moment forever. All too quickly, though, I was back in the game, aware of the crowd and everyone around me yelling, clapping, cheering — and all for me.

That was the only time I ever felt my father's approval.

Off-Season Basketball

Here's how I'm going to beat you. I'm going to outwork you.
That's it. That's all there is to it.

—Pat Summit

Pat Summit has been another source of inspiration to me over the years. She was a Tennessee powerhouse coach and tireless advocate for women's basketball. I have had great coaches over the course of my life in sports, and I have also worked hard for my successes.

I started playing basketball when I was ten. One of my closest friends, Caryn Sackman, had played since she was little. She basically recruited me so we could do it together. Caryn was a tomboy, tall for her age, and well known for her basketball skills. We were both strong and skinny, with big hands and feet, and by the time we turned twelve, we were five feet, seven inches tall. They called us the Twin Towers because no one could get over us! We played hard, but we had so much fun.

Dad encouraged me to play basketball because he thought it would be excellent off-season training for soccer. He also knew I could use my goalkeeping skills to get hold of the ball. He was right on both counts. But it was Ken Sackman, Caryn's dad, who coached us a few years in rec basketball during our middle school years.

Ken made sure I used my height to my best advantage, and that I never stood still, constantly yelling from the coach's box, "Don't grow roots!" I use that line myself now when I coach basketball. It's a brilliant line.

Learning from Basketball Hall of Famers

After our move to Georgia years later, I got to meet two Basketball Hall of Famers, Katrina McClain Johnson and Teresa Edwards.

Katrina McClain Johnson is a two-time Olympic Gold Medalist and a record-setting Lady Bulldog at the University of Georgia (UGA) from 1983 to 1987. She had an incredible career playing on many USA basketball teams, including three Olympic teams. I knew her as Aunty Kat.

Teresa Edwards—Aunty T to me—was a four-time Olympic

Gold Medalist who also began her career at UGA. She became the youngest athlete to win an Olympic gold medal in women's basketball at the 1984 Los Angeles Olympic Games. Teresa was also inducted into the Naismith Memorial Basketball Hall of Fame, and as I look at her pictures today, she looks the same to me as she did back then.

Dad facilitated a visit from both phenomenal athletes to our high school in rural Gainesville, Georgia, during a basketball practice session. They spent time with us, worked some drills together, and really fostered a team-bonding mindset. It was a fantastic opportunity from which we benefited enormously.

Baseball and Being Kids

I played softball, but baseball was one of my favorite sports to watch, live and on TV. Baseball has always been a relaxing downtime for me, maybe because it was a favorite family pastime in LA. We had season tickets to the LA Dodgers games, thanks to my dad's job. Dodger Stadium had the Diamond Vision giant screen made by his company and behind home plate, about four rows back were their corporate seats.

Ken Sackman had seats down the first baseline, and he taught us how to keep score in those fancy programs they used to give out. I will never forget when I was in the fourth or fifth grade, the Braves were in town playing the Dodgers, and Ken Sackman took Caryn (Sackman), Jack Rosenfeld, and me to the game.

For some reason (pretty sure it was Jack's idea), we singled out David Justice to harass *relentlessly*. He was an up-and-coming right fielder for the Braves, and every time he was out there playing defense, we shouted, "Dave Justice, you suck!" We did that for *hours*. Bless his heart, he put up with it for a long time, but finally, he got so frustrated that he took his mitt off, walked over to us, and said, "Look, you wanna try?" We were all like, "Yes! Yes!"

Stats and the Psychology of Sports Betting

I'm also a huge professional sports better, especially with football. My father taught me about March Madness when I was very young, which is all about the NCAA Men's Division I tournament in college basketball. We cheered for UCLA, but Dad got me to understand local and professional sports teams. My local college team was USC, and my professional team was the Rams.

Understanding stats and the chance factor involved excited me, and I had fun rooting for teams about which I knew nothing. I loved the obscure teams, underdogs like the Central Michigan Chippewas, and would find loopholes, study them, and often win. Somehow, despite studying sports stats more than school subjects in high school, my grades were pretty good.

I also bet on fantasy sports. Some baseball games too, but baseball is more about loving the sport and watching it from the perspective of the pitch. I focus on two things: the pitch count and the bullpen. Specifically, how the ball leaves the pitcher's hand and the line it takes to the strike zone at home plate for the batter to do whatever it is they're going to do with it.

There's a psychology behind the pitch that has fascinated me since I was little. Whether it's a hit, a miss, or a pitch that was so good that the pitcher controlled it to pop up, the psychology is significant.

The pitcher is constantly reading cues from the batter and has probably watched tape on him. He's always thinking of how to strike him out and reading signals from the catcher, all while giving nothing away in his facial expressions or body movements. The pitcher's mound is the loneliest place in baseball because he's always in his own head—that quicksand thing.

Checking Tape

Dad was also big on checking tape. People record games a lot to study their performance in any sport to see where they can improve. They look at things like swing, hand placement, stance, everything. Watching recordings to learn from them is a highly beneficial tool when handled correctly. My dad didn't.

From my perspective today as a parent and a coach, I want to say that if the parent speaks in a derogatory way or hounds the child, it isn't conducive to the outcome the parent wants.

For example, if the child can observe their stance, it can be a collaborative effort between parent and child. "Do you see what you're doing with your foot? What do you think would happen if you rotate on the ball of your foot?" The child can discover it for themselves; learning can take place, confidence grows, skills improve, and everyone wins.

And at the end of the day, your feet should be dirty,
your hair messy and your eyes sparkling.

—Shanti

7

The Summer of '94

T he summer of 1994 heralded, among other world events, my family's cross-country move from the metropolitan city of Los Angeles, California, to the then-rural community of Gainesville, Georgia, about fifty-five miles northeast of Atlanta. My parents had made the executive decision to send me off to a sleepaway camp for the month while the rest of the family relocated, effectively taking me and my bad attitude out of the equation. A wise choice, my being, at the time, an angst-filled teenager with zero interest in the move.

Camp Agawak

I had spent two previous summers at Camp Agawak, a girls' camp dedicated to the development of young ladies ages seven to sixteen. Then, when I was twelve, LAUSD (the LA Unified School District) gave year-round school a go. This meant we only had six weeks of summer but two months of winter break. That ended my Midwest sleepaway camp experience until 1994.

Camp Agawak. You'll find it in Minocqua, a small, friendly lake town in the beautiful Northwoods of Wisconsin. Across the lake is the boys' camp, Kawaga, which is our camp's name spelled backward. Or, as they liked to say, spelled correctly. We vigorously disagreed!

Maple, aspen, northern red oak, basswood, and red and white

pine trees dominate the northern forests of Wisconsin. Some of them towered over the camp and lake like giant skyscrapers. The fresh scent of sappy pine trees, and the feel of pinecones crunching and pine straw smashing under our sneakers, are still vivid memories.

Small, unseen forest creatures made quick, little sounds as they chattered with each other or raced to hide from our approach. In the early mornings, the lake was smooth and still, like a mirror. Hot, humid days and cool nights created a layer of steam over the lake that was both eerie and inviting, just sitting there at first, then rolling around in gentle circles until finally dissipating as the morning wore on.

Agawak is where I learned a lot of exciting, new, and wonderfully addictive activities. Things like water skiing, broadcasting in their own radio station, and, of course, gossip. The whole camp culture, with its songs and sayings, always extended into my return home every year. I entertained my family when I got back, partly because I missed it so much, and partly because I wanted them to love it as much as I did.

My First Year at Camp

I was nine years old the first time I attended Agawak. Mom picked me up from school a few hours before summer break officially began, and after saying good-bye to my friends, we headed to LAX Airport. Back then, my mother could come to the gate to help me, an unaccompanied minor, get situated on the plane.

The flight attendants were very nice, making sure I had my snacks and was comfy in my seat. An older man with extremely unsavory breath sat next to me on the flight. Fortunately, I had a bag of peppermints in my snack stash, so I used the opportunity to introduce myself and ask if he'd like one. He didn't tell me his name, but he did accept a mint. Goal achieved.

Aunt Esther, my mom's sister, claimed me when we landed in

Chicago. I spent the night with her and Uncle Chuck in Highland Park, Illinois. All my necessities for the month were packed into two giant duffle bags and one trunk. The bags were so big a person could easily fit in one if they scrunched up a little. The next day, a worker from the camp picked me up and we began our nearly five-hour commute to the camp, my stuff safely stowed away in the back of his giant blue SUV.

I don't know if that's how they usually got campers up to Agawak or if that was something special they offered those of us arriving from outside the regular camp bus route, but it was great. The driver was attractive, even to a nine-year-old. His vehicle smelled like male cologne, and he may have been a closet smoker, as there was a faint lingering scent of cigarettes. Once there, life as I knew it would never be the same.

Camp Culture

The culture at Camp Agawak was probably fairly typical as those things go, but it was a whole new world for me and the other girls. The camp has been in existence since 1921, so many of them were multigenerational camp attendees.

Each screened-in cabin housed six to nine young ladies, grouped by age. You'd walk into a large area with bunk beds, and in the back was a tiny water closet that housed a toilet and a sink. The cabins also had a connected counselor's area, a small room with a bunk bed. They were all on one side of the campus, scattered on a hill. The showers and larger bathrooms, plus the mess hall and a few other buildings, were on the other side of the campus, along either side of a trail.

Some of the staff and assistant counselors were as young as fifteen, but most were college-age or in their twenties. They helped us break down the weekly chores for each cabin and prepare for inspections every morning after breakfast and before activities. Everyone had to make their bed, help mop the floor, and tidy the bathroom. Many of the girls had never had to do chores before, so they learned how to dust, mop, and so on. But everyone got into it because it was a team effort, and more to the point, there were winners for the cleanest cabin.

There were some less than fun "accolades" to be had as well. One of them was getting a pair of your undies stolen during the night and waking up for morning assembly at the flagpole to find them flying there for all to experience. Most things at camp were just good fun and provided a time for bonding; and they did this, too, as a good-natured prank.

Each cabin had someone assigned as a food server for their cabinmates. When it was our turn, we'd go up to the giant window with all the kitchen staff behind it, picking up and dropping off dishes, pitchers of water and juice, and enjoying lots of smiles. The phrase "You kill it, you fill it" came from camp. I brought that one home, and it went over . . . semi-well.

We learned how to scrape plates clean into giant buckets, then dump the buckets into a massive hole in the forest. That part wasn't much fun, but everyone contributed and took a turn or two.

I made friends with the kitchen staff every year. Most of them were return seasonal employees and probably loved watching us—well, at least some of us—grow up. The kinder we were to any staff, the more rewards we'd reap—rewards like extra desserts, larger portions, or better cuts of whatever they were serving. It was a great lesson, and I may have missed the point then, but looking back, I can acknowledge the life lessons.

Lady Godiva

My first year at camp at nine was also the first time I ever went skinny-dipping. It was on an all-girls overnight camping trip while at Camp Agawak. There were no sexual undertones to it, just a feeling of *liberation*. It was almost as if the entire cabin had hit a wall of camp nonsense and we just wanted to free ourselves, be ourselves, and live in the purest moment right then.

Buck-naked, splashing each other in the cool air, and floating around in warm, fairly shallow water, as it was dark and we were, after all, still sensible young ladies. I'm sure the counselor assigned to our cabin was freaking out, but we felt like powerful little Lady Godivas coming into our own.

While I didn't immediately make lifelong friends through camp, some of those friends came roaring back into play later as an adult, and we are all friendly to this day. Since I was the only camper from California, they dubbed me "CA," so I was a bit of a camp celebrity that first and second year. But I soon found out that a lot had changed during my absence.

People Change

My first day back as a fourteen-year-old was a huge letdown. I recognized the girls from back when we were nine who had attended summer camp every year since. I was super excited to see them until I quickly realized they had grown into mean, insecure, spoiled young women who had established a pecking order during the years I'd missed. I wanted to be friends with everyone, but the popular girls, my former nine-year-old friends, had their own clique, and I didn't fit in anymore.

That summer was rough. I was now on the outside of the popular crew, with no real friends, feeling inadequate for the first time in my life. But then, there was one girl in particular. From the first time I met this girl at nine, the other girls were making fun of her and treating her differently. I didn't participate, but I also didn't stop them, which I still regret.

But now we were fourteen, both outcasts, and I felt a keen sense of loneliness. During open activities one day, I wanted to swim and dive at the lakefront. Darcy was heading that way too, so I said hi in a friendly voice. Her reaction was very disheartening. She seemed confused when I addressed her, because, as I'd noticed, no one really spoke to her that summer. I thought, *At least people speak to me, dang.*

Darcy was clearly lonely too, so I asked if she wanted to go for a swim together, and she lit up immediately. She said she'd go get the scuba gear for us, but then turned back to me and said, "Don't leave!" I smiled and said, "Okay, I won't." She started to leave again, but then turned around *again* to say, "Seriously, don't leave." That broke my heart!

The poor girl came to this camp summer after summer, clearly because her parents forced her, not because she wanted to come. Why would she when the others treated her like dirt every summer? And here I was, legitimately interested in spending time with her, and she thought I might prank her.

We had a great time that day.

Blue vs. White

Camp-wide Color War (Blues against the Whites) had become *the* thing. I don't remember it being that big of a deal when we were nine and it was called "Capture the Flag." But this year, the whole camp went insane for it. They split the entire camper population down the middle, each team comprising campers of all ages. Everyone had to participate in at least one event for it to count as a team effort.

This year, I was on the Blue team. The counselors nominated the team captains, which seemed odd to everyone. They nominated me, and trust me when I say that the popular girls were not pleased. In retrospect, it's clear that the staff knew what they were doing.

Agawak devoted the final few days of camp to Color War. I heard that a huge soccer competition closed everything out, so I immediately wrote to my dad, begging him to overnight my soccer gear as soon as he got the letter. I explained it was my only opportunity to prove myself to these girls. Soccer was my best sport, and as a skilled goalkeeper, I knew I could keep our team from getting scored on for the win.

My father already knew I wasn't enjoying myself there that

year. The staff had allowed me to call him earlier because, much like Darcy, I was miserable, and I wanted to go home. Dad, however, wanted me to stick it out, so when he got my letter, he wanted to support me and boost my confidence. He knew my strength in soccer and that I could help the team win, so he immediately sent my gear. Game time came, I kept the goal clear of any scoring, and we *destroyed* the White team. Yes!

Even though it was the end of the session, coming together like that was worth it. It turned out to be the best day I'd had at camp that summer. Because of Darcy, it was also my first real lesson in authenticity, staying true to yourself and to what you know in your heart is right.

It's a Small World after All

Many moons later, as an adult and a parent, my neighbor and I were catching up on things as we pushed our kids on her swing set. Somehow, we got onto the topic of camps, and as we shared our experiences, we realized they were quite similar. I started singing an Agawak camp song that only another Agawak girl would recognize and watched her face light up as she joined in with me!

Although we came from opposite sides of the country and had attended different sessions at Agawak, we had all the same friends. We all keep in touch to this day.

It really is a small world.

All Good Things Must Come to an End

That was my last year at Camp Agawak, and I was glad it had ended on a happy note. Up till now, I'd been able to put the thought of my family's move across the country out of my mind. Now that camp was over, I returned to my aunt and uncle's home in Chicago, and from there not back home to LA, but on to my new life in Georgia.

Change is inevitable. Growth is optional.

—John C. Maxwell

* 8 *

Starting Over in Georgia

My mom met me at the Atlanta airport and drove us to the Atlanta suburb of Gainesville. Not having any idea what to expect was nerve-racking, and it's that drive from the airport I remember most from the entire trip. We came out of the airport, heading north on I-85 to the bypass and onto the north side of I-285. As I later learned, that put us "outside the perimeter," or OTP.

Once OTP, the buildings suddenly disappeared, and I went from a familiar city landscape to what seemed like nothingness, only fields and cows. There were no familiar, welcoming city smells of hot concrete and car exhaust fumes, only new and strange country smells of chicken farms, cow patties, and the occasional skunk. I had never seen or smelled anything like it before in my life, not even at camp.

Ultimately, the move changed my life in ways I couldn't imagine, but at the time, I only knew I was leaving my comfortable, familiar life and friends behind, maybe forever, and I was terrified.

First Impressions

Our new home was set back a third of a mile from the road. Mom said that if you walked it, by the time you got to the house, the day would have changed significantly because it took so long. The driveway snaked back and forth like the Amazon River, up a hill, past several pastures, a horse barn, a riding arena, a swimming pool, and a tennis court. It finally ended in a large parking area with a carport next to the house. The carport thing was new too. I was used to seeing garages or street parking in LA, but I mostly saw ranch houses with carports here in Georgia.

And instead of the small yard back in LA, we were now nestled inside forty-four acres of our very own, an unimaginable expanse. Ginger, our twelve-year-old golden lab, had never smelled anything remotely like the Southern countryside either, and she was busy happily exploring her new surroundings. I suspect the move added at least an extra year to her life. She had begun having bi-weekly strokes, and my mother, with great compassion, finally had her put down two years later. But for now, she was thoroughly enjoying herself.

Everyone else was excited about the move. My brother, Stephen, had spent the four weeks I was away at camp chasing frogs, jumping in and out of creeks, and making shirtless friends. Apparently, country boys don't wear shirts in the summer heat—news to me. It was also the first time Stephen had ever seen fireflies in his own backyard. We didn't have fireflies in LA, and the sheer number of insects overall was astonishing.

With a few weeks to go before school started, Stephen continued to have fun and tried to share his excitement with me. I wasn't interested, however, and spent the time moping around with an attitude. I did get my room organized the way I wanted it, but the rest of the time, I slept in, tanned by the pool, and rolled my eyes at everyone as I avoided responsibilities as best I could.

Farmer Dad and Country Life

Imagine a five-foot-seven, uber-professional attorney, all decked out in brand-new, crisply pressed denim overalls, ready to mow a lawn for the first time in his life—on a riding mower, mind you—and you've just pictured my dad. I'm not 100 percent sure he had his thumbs tucked into his suspenders, but he may have.

And by lawn, I mean rural country grass that's miles long, and it grew all along both sides of our *Forrest Gump*-like driveway. Dad knew there was an art to mowing, so he was trying to figure it out. I didn't know you could put so much time and effort into cutting grass.

One time, he accidentally mowed over a wasp's nest. We were all inside the house watching him mow when we saw him suddenly leap from the mower, waving his arms wildly, run to the pool, and dive in. It looked hilarious, and we laughed till we cried.

When he finally came in, soaking wet and pissed, he asked, "Did you see that?" probably desperately hoping we hadn't. That got us all going again, to which he responded, "Not funny." Fortunately for my father, his quick action worked, and he escaped that incident unharmed.

Our home was more like a permanent summer camp. We'd acquired two horses and had a neighboring donkey named Jenny. Jenny had a serious attitude problem, probably why I liked her. I have since learned that a female donkey is called a "jenny." There you go.

Another neighbor had six cows that invariably escaped, apparently for the sole purpose of hanging out in our driveway. We also had a septic tank to learn how to deal with and trash that had to be taken to the dump; new experiences for all of us.

Jewish Faith in the Bible Belt

Part of the settling-in process involved finding a temple for the upcoming fall Jewish holidays, so we ventured over to Athens, Georgia, to attend the Congregation Children of Israel. We ended up joining, and I was later confirmed, and my brother had his bar mitzvah there. The rabbi introduced us to the rest of the "Gainesville Crew," as he called them. The Berzacks and the

Cohens were members who became my parents' best friends, and I am still friends with them today.

Making new friends and dating in the Bible Belt was completely different from what I was used to back in LA. Religion was a huge issue here. For one thing, in Georgia, dating meant that you might end up together, so it was important to parents that their Christian kids date other Christian kids. So later, when I started dating Jason, he shared his faith with me. He wanted me to become a Christian so we could keep dating. I just wanted to attend homecoming together, but his parents didn't think it was a good idea. He ended up asking a freshman instead, and it devastated me.

My Jewish faith was also an issue in forming friendships—not in a bad way, but from the standpoint of my new friends sincerely caring about me and not wanting me to go to hell. They weren't obnoxious about it, just talked with me or left pamphlets in my locker. The Southern Baptists pushed it more than the Presbyterians and the Methodists, and they were sincere in their belief and attempts to convince me.

My parents disagreed on how to handle what Christians call "witnessing" to me, that is, explaining what they believed. They believe we are all sinners in need of salvation, that Jesus was the promised Messiah, the Son of G-d, the only one who can forgive sins, and the only way to Heaven, and that forgiveness is freely given to all who ask for it.

My mother wanted me to avoid them altogether, but my father wanted it to play out naturally. Then I got an opportunity to go to a Billy Graham brigade when the twins, Sonny and Sally, especially Sonny, urged me to go. I knew them from band, where Sonny played tuba and Sally was a percussionist. In true form, Mom didn't want me to go, and Dad left the decision up to me, so I went.

My Christian friends wanted me to go so I would get "saved" (saved from hell) at the rally. I didn't understand that concept. In Judaism, we have Yom Kippur, our yearly holy day, to pray for our sins. But I went to see what it was all about and to be social.

We knew people from other high schools who said they were saved, even though they were having premarital sex, drinking, and doing drugs, things I knew Christians weren't supposed to do. I finally told one of my new Christian friends, "Hey, don't worry about it, man. Jews don't believe in hell." So, after that event, they did not approach me anymore about converting to Christianity.

It's important to know what you believe in and stand up for it.

The KKK in Gainesville

Having a KKK Grand Wizard living less than a mile away from us was a big concern for my parents. In case you don't know, the Ku Klux Klan is not a religion. It's a horribly prejudiced, White, southern group formed after the Civil War in resistance to the Republican Party's policies to abolish slavery and establish political and economic equality for Black Americans.

My father's family had lost loved ones in the Holocaust, so they knew firsthand about prejudice and persecution. While we never became direct targets, the group held a few rallies in town over the years, even going door-to-door with their hateful leaflets on at least one occasion I can recall.

They didn't have an overpowering presence while I attended Johnson High, but my mom told me the class after mine was very excited about the KKK coming back stronger than ever. I'm glad I missed that. Mom, with her characteristically dry sense of humor, mentioned it in a letter to the Walkers after I'd left for college, which Katie recently passed along to me:

> For a little local color, we had a KKK rally in town. It was attended by 200 protesters and eight clansmen. I had the misfortune of seeing one of them in his garb on the corner of my street handing out leaflets the week prior.

It was not a pleasant sight . . . I calmly checked with my local friends and was told not to be concerned. Jews were not on the hit list, just Blacks and Hispanics. How comforting. They only invited White Christians to their rally, so I did not attend.

The Woman in Dana's Bed

I met Melanie in the summer of 1998. We were both eighteen and I was home from school, working at a popular sports bar. Melanie was away on vacation, and while she was gone, I slept with her boyfriend, Shane. She heard the rumors and confronted me about it when she got back. I replied honestly that I had slept with him, but I didn't know they were a thing at the time. Shane didn't tell me, nor did anyone else.

She liked my honesty, so she hatched a plan to surprise Shane by having us both show up on his doorstep to hang out. You should have seen his face! Still, Melanie and Shane stayed together that summer, and the three of us had a great time as friends. Melanie and I have been inseparable ever since.

Melanie and I spent a lot of time hanging out and tanning by our pool. I was still lifeguarding some during the day and working at the sports bar in the evening. Then, after closing, we would head over to Atlanta to party and club. That's when she started calling me her "bodyguard," because she was five feet, three inches and I was almost six feet tall.

My mother's only rule was that I had to come home at night. One night, Melanie and I stayed out very late and didn't get back to my place until around four a.m. She didn't want to drive the extra half hour to her house, so she crashed with me in my bed.

Three hours later, my mother, always the drama queen, burst through my door barking orders for the day. I was still out of it with so little sleep, but I tried to introduce her to Melanie since she was sleeping right next to me, but Mom was in and out of the room too quickly.

A few minutes later she called me on the phone, yelling, wanting to know whose car was in our driveway and did I have a boy in bed with me? I laughed and told her I had tried to introduce them, but she probably couldn't see Melanie because she was so tiny and Mom's view from the doorway hid her. Then, seconds later, she burst back into the room, just to make sure there was no boy in bed with me.

Mom must have called her sister and all her girlfriends to tell them the story. My family still tells it to this day, referring to Melanie as "the Woman in Dana's Bed." This is also how my mom and Melanie started their friendship. When I was away at school, the two of them would hang out, not much and not every day, but Melanie liked Mom's maternal side, and Mom liked to know what I was up to.

Mel and I avoided a lot of potentially serious trouble that summer, and what we got into, we are taking with us to the grave!

Hairstyles change, and skirt lengths, and slang,
but high school administration? Never.

—Stephen King

9

The High School Years

My standard wake-up time was around noon over the course of that first summer in Gainesville. One morning, my father got me up earlier to go to my new high school and meet the band director. I played tenor saxophone since sixth grade in middle school band back in LA and planned on joining band here too.

Intro to the Band

We headed out to Johnson High School and found the marching band practicing on what looked like a practice football field. They were a marching band during football season, and for the rest of the school year, winter and spring, they were a concert band.

It was a typically hot and muggy summer day in Georgia, and all fifty-five to sixty members were in shorts and T-shirts. I met the band director, David (Doc) Jones, the kindest person I'd ever met. This being the last day of band camp, they'd already memorized the marching moves along with the music, and there was only one more practice scheduled for that evening. Doc invited me to come back and learn the music then, which I did.

That evening, I memorized the music, we played as a unit, and then broke off into sectional work. This is where I first met Casey, my tenor saxophone section leader. We had to play a C with a little vibrato. Casey hadn't heard me play before, and when he did, I knew I'd won him over.

The band had cool marching uniforms that included hats with plumage in our school colors, baby blue and white. I officially signed up, and once school started, we began practices after school hours, when we worked on getting the formations down. During the day in class, we did a lot of the memorization work. I was also a jazz band and pep band member until I made varsity basketball my sophomore year.

First Day of High School

My first day of school was much easier than it might have been, had I not already made friends through band practice. That morning, I got ready to head out to the bus with my hair tied back in a ponytail, dressed in black combat boots, oversized and baggy suspender pants (charcoal gray with a white pinstripe), and a white button-down, oversized shirt. That completed the pseudo-professional look I was going for.

"You're going to wear that?" demanded my father.

"Yup," I replied confidently. "*And* I'm gonna make friends with the first Black person I meet. Bye!"

And with that, I got on the bus.

My aunts and cousins told me many years later that I always knew what I wanted and would always get it. "When you were little and you wanted to play on that swing, that's exactly what you did." How right they were.

High School Sports and Earning Respect

I soon realized that the commitment to sports at my new school was at a whole new level. AAU (Amateur Athletic Union) was all summer long, so sports dominated my extracurricular activities. I was a fairly good kid in high school simply because I didn't have time to be anything else.

At first, I didn't have much respect for my basketball team.

They didn't understand critical concepts that I had learned, like "space," and the team was pretty disconnected. But by the end of the season, we had melded into a cohesive, powerful unit and we were *invincible*. Camaraderie is what every coach prays for, and that mutual trust and friendship extends very nicely into the rest of one's life.

Later, during the practice session in which Aunty Kat (Katrina McClain Johnson) and Aunty T (Teresa Edwards) coached us, I was still proving myself to the other girls on the team. Knowing these basketball legends didn't win everyone over. It impressed Kathy, but not enough to convince her I was a worthy player.

While I'd made varsity in my high school sophomore year, Kathy had made it in junior high. She was strong, an excellent guard with major handling skills. Kathy also had excellent peripheral vision and could see passing lanes. I didn't gain her respect until I proved my skills in game situations with her.

My years of experience with goalkeeping in soccer was an immense advantage, and with my height and strong hands, I could catch and score, or pass, appropriately. Dad never coached me in basketball, but he encouraged me and gave me some good advice. "Use your height and your skilled hands to your advantage. If you can catch her stuff, she can trust you." But Kathy was a tough nut to crack. Even after proving I could handle her passes, it wasn't enough. It took more for us to make a genuine connection.

Kathy was a beautiful girl with a short, cute, boyish haircut. The girls' hairstyle in Gainesville at the time was straight hair with an asymmetrical cut. Kids—people—can be cruel, and because she was tomboyish and had short hair, some guys called her Kevin. I didn't appreciate it, so I stood up for her and told them not to talk about my teammate. I still have no patience for that kind of thing, and I'm loyal to a fault. Well, Kathy heard about it and gave me a brief nod in the hall. After that, we had what I like to think was a mutual understanding and respect for each other.

SAT Pressure

I took an SAT prep class in the spring of 1997, my junior year in high school. According to my dad, I failed miserably on my first attempt at the SAT exam with a score of 980. That summer I was dating Billy, who went to the same high school and was a fellow lifeguard at the Lake Lanier Island Water Park. Since I did poorly on the exam, Dad grounded me from dating. At first, I could keep the lifeguarding job, but I had to study SAT prep four hours every day.

That didn't go over very well with me, so I continued to date Billy. But one morning we got busted. Billy had gotten away with sneaking through my window dozens of times before, but this time we'd fallen asleep until six a.m., and the neighbors saw him leaving that morning. They told my parents, so my mom had to speak with his mom, and it was bad. But to us, it was young love.

After that, my father grounded me hardcore. I had to quit my lifeguarding job and stop seeing Billy and *all* my friends, other than seeing them at school that fall. He also made me study SAT prep *eight* hours each day, because he didn't think I was showing enough improvement.

That's when I became seriously depressed, as I realize now, and contemplated suicide for the first and only time in my life. I removed a razor blade from one of my pink, disposable razors, sat on the bathroom floor, and slowly and painfully dragged the razor's edge across the skin of my left wrist. Thankfully, I soon realized that this was not what I really wanted. In the end, no one knew how I felt or what I'd been experiencing.

I've kept this suicide attempt a secret from everyone — until now.

SAT Relief

I plugged along that summer until my senior year began in the fall. I'd retaken the SAT test and the results came back. My father shared them with me after a marching band halftime performance, away from everyone else. We went over by the concession stand he and my mother worked that evening as Band Booster Club copresidents, something they were very involved in.

I'd gotten a 1200—600, and 600, dead even. Dad admitted he'd hoped for better scores, but he wasn't totally disappointed. He said the results would get me into the colleges he wanted me to apply to. He also told me I was being recruited for Division I soccer, oh by the way.

The pressure dam broke, and as relief flooded over and through me, I sobbed on his shoulder. It was finally over. I didn't have to take the SATs ever again, the grounding was over, and I could live my life again.

I went to my first concert in my senior year, where we saw the Wallflowers and Counting Crows. My good friend Cindy and I got our parents' permission to drive into Atlanta together for a live show at Chastain Park Amphitheater, a wonderfully unique outdoor venue, small and intimate.

After that experience, I couldn't wait to leave Gainesville behind and begin my new, independent life in Atlanta.

Recruited!

Both Florida State University (FSU) and the University of Georgia (UGA) recruited me in soccer. I'd also applied to Agnes Scott College, a private women's institution for which I had *zero* interest in attending, but I did it to appease my father.

We drove down to FSU to meet the band director and the soccer coach. I wanted to be a music major and a high school band director like Doc Jones. But soccer and marching band were the same seasons in college, and neither coach would give an inch on missing practices. So FSU was out, but I kept all the cool swag they gave me.

UGA it was, and I was going to be a DAWG. I went to the audition for a chair in the band, but when I saw the saxophone professor who was trying me out, I turned around and walked right back out. It was the same guy who, throughout high school, was consistently demeaning in his behavior toward me. He made fun of everything I did from the way I cleaned and packed my saxophone, to the way I played it. And it wasn't just with me.

No surprise that I took that ongoing criticism back then. Not only was I conditioned to take it but in that region of the country, it wasn't acceptable to talk back to people in authority. This time? Nope! Not happening. My father was furious, but I stuck to my guns.

As it turned out, the day we were leaving for FSU, I received a letter of acceptance from ASC (Agnes Scott College) with a nice little academic scholarship included. I was going to be a Scottie after all. Best four years I could have asked for in a college experience!

I was moving the hell away from "Gainsvegas," as the locals had nicknamed it, to a *real* city, as I saw it, with unlimited possibilities.

Summer will end soon enough, and childhood as well.

—George R. R. Martin

10

Summer Interlude

T he summer of 1998 marked my high school graduation and the promise of a new beginning at Agnes Scott College in the fall.

We had planned to visit Europe that summer, all of us together as a family. But then Mom got a severe case of sciatica, so I figured she couldn't go. Also, Dad had just gotten a brand-new sports car, so he wasn't going. And if Dad wasn't going, I wasn't either. So, naturally, I thought they would shelve the trip.

Surprise! Mom and Stephen went by themselves. This is an excerpt from her January 1999 letter to the Walkers:

David and Dana stayed home to work and feed the animals. Not terribly exciting, but it was their choice.

It didn't seem that way to me, but regardless, it left Dad and me to fend for ourselves. When he wasn't working, he was having fun with his new sports car, and I was lifeguarding and working at the sports bar.

That was a World Cup year. Not all bars broadcast all the games, so sometimes my father would come up to watch one at my bar. It was great to see him . . . at first. Until he would start with the close inspection and tell me privately, in French, "Watch your eyes! Watch your facial expressions!"

He said the looks I gave could kill; that when I cut my eyes at someone, they felt it. He wanted me to have a neutral expression and smile more to hide my feelings. According to my husband, I still lack in the Poker Face realm. Anyway, by then I was totally ready for my father to leave.

Bread, Cheese, and Apples—Again?

Dad wanted me to come home for dinner every night. Correction: he wanted me to come home and *cook* dinner every night, which was interesting because neither of us knew how to cook.

So for two weeks, we lived on various cheeses, crusty French bread, and apples until we couldn't stand it any longer. And I think we were becoming malnourished! That's when Dad started picking up "Harry's in a Hurry" from Harry's Grocery Store, prepared, packaged dinners for that week's meals. Much better.

That's how we survived until Mom and Stephen came home from their summer European jaunt. Here's how she described it:

In March, I managed to crush my sciatica nerve while horseback riding and suffered through painkillers, steroids, and acupuncture until June. By then I felt well enough to take Stevie on a six-week backpacking trip to Europe. We visited friends and relatives and places I had never been to. We had the best time together.

Stevie soaked in all the history and was able to take world history his first semester of freshman year and aced it. He would like to be a history major but is worried about getting a job! He also managed to pick up a few girls here and there in that universal language of his and even found us some new friends in Spain who live not too far from us in Georgia.

The deal we made was he would visit all castles, museums, etc. No Louvre, Prado, etc. We saw Les Misérables *in London and Shakespeare's* As You Like It *at the Globe, and spent lots of time in Paris, Brittany, and Normandy. We went to the WWII beaches and the American cemetery, learned all about William the Conqueror, and saw authentic Viking ships in Denmark.*

We took all modes of transport except roller skates. We cruised the Rhine, biked in Germany and Copenhagen, sailed the canals in Amsterdam on my nephew's little boat, and the usual cars, trains, and planes.

It was an extraordinary adventure that will stay with us forever.

That summer passed quickly. Athletes were required to report to their new dorms at Agnes Scott four to six weeks early to begin conditioning for upcoming fall sports. I was ready. I broke up with Billy, packed up all my stuff, and for the most part, didn't look back.

Why do you go away? So that you can come back. So that you can see the place you came from with new eyes and extra colors. And the people there see you differently, too. Coming back to where you started is not the same as never leaving.

—Terry Pratchett

* 11 *

Agnes Scott College

T he fall of 1998 was rife with the promise of great things to come. I had graduated from Johnson High School and was preparing to live away from home and the stifling, small town of Gainesville. I could finally spread my wings and live a *real* life at my new school, Agnes Scott College, close to the thriving metropolitan city of Atlanta.

Agnes Scott College is a private women's liberal arts school in Decatur, Georgia, serving undergraduate and graduate students. Considered one of the Seven Sisters of the South, the institution has a history of turning out remarkable women, like Jennifer Nettles, singer/songwriter; Saycon Sengbloh, actress/singer; and Wasfia Nazreen, mountaineer, environmentalist, and writer. The campus itself is breathtaking, with gorgeous old brick buildings, flying buttresses, and quad areas with the greenest grass you've ever seen.

Freshman Friends

The school places incoming freshmen together as roommates, and from my perspective, they did an outstanding job that year. Little did I know that my freshman year roommate, Sara, would be my roommate for the next eleven *years*. We are still great friends today, with only two semi-serious disagreements along the way.

We had a strong core group of friends that year: Sara, Laura, Erin, Monique, Kathy, Beth, Jenny who was on our hall that year, and me. The group dwindled as girls transferred, failed out, or made friends elsewhere, but Sara, Erin, Monique, Laura, and I are still close friends today. Students established groups and cliques very early on, but I tried not to limit myself to one group.

I had moved into my freshman dorm six weeks early, along with the other fall sports players, so there were no issues to deal with in that regard. Mom, Dad, and Stephen were in my dorm room lovingly unpacking my clothes, towels, bedding, and other things when in walked a tiny, adorable, friendly young woman.

She introduced herself as Alice. She noticed my Star of David around my neck and immediately walked over to me and flung her arms around me. Alice held me in a long, tight hug and said in a voice filled with emotion, "I thought you were all dead."

I looked at my parents and brother as they stared at this stranger embracing me. We were all like, *WTF?* It turned out she'd been taught in school that all the Jews died in the Holocaust. We had a few discussions about that later. Today, Alice holds a PhD in urban planning and public policy and a master's in industrial-organizational psychology. She's a swimmer and outdoor enthusiast, a brilliant human being, and an all-around great person.

Winship and Walters

We were in the Winship dorm, and at the time, there was a bit of rivalry between us and Walters, another freshman dorm. Walters housed a sizable group of my soccer buddies. My friend Mary was there, along with Betty, a sixteen-year-old prodigy. They introduced us to their friends, Kourtney, Susan, and Callie—a tight-knit group of ladies, all still friends to this day.

Walters was generally considered nicer than Winship, but Winship had more drama. I'm thinking of a few girls who had eating disorders. I remember walking into some of their bathrooms and smelling the vomit they had saved in their bathtubs.

These were significant health concerns, and some of those young ladies soon left college to deal with their underlying insecurities, growing pains, or hidden disabilities. These kinds of health issues are stereotypical of women, but they became a reality to those of us who had never seen anything like it before.

"Man on the Hall!"

On a lighter note, Agnes Scott had a few unique freshman-year rules, such as no overnight stays for boys. Yeah, right. So, during night fire drills, guys would sneak out dressed in robes or towels to disguise themselves, as if they were fooling anyone.

Another rule was that when a man, any man, came into any hall, he had to shout "man on the hall!" Most of the guys loved that one.

College Sports

At ASC, I played three Division III sports: soccer, basketball, and softball. Monique and I played basketball and softball together and became close through the beautiful team camaraderie. The girls would come to all my home games and cheer me on. When my dad attended, he would request a particular cheer from them. "Do the Spirit thing!" he'd always ask.

The Spirit cheer went like this: "We've got spirit, S-P-I-R-I-T, Let's hear it!" with accompanying hand movements and claps. They loved doing it for Dad. My nickname was Deez, short for Deez Nutz, popular back then, so they'd start the cheer out softly, gradually getting louder and louder, quietly slipping in the "Nutz" so my dad wouldn't hear.

Coach Mac was the assistant basketball coach, and I had a massive crush on him. To my delight, he took me out in my senior year, and I thought that was going to be *it*. But instead, it turned out to be more of a pseudo-adult pep talk, encouraging me to have more respect and confidence in myself because I could do great things. He was a great mentor, and when I started coaching professionally later in life, he was very proud of me. We keep in touch, and he is always positive and uplifting.

In soccer, I had a great coaching mentor in Coach Luca. I butted heads with her a bit during my freshman year because she pushed me so hard. What I did not understand then was her renowned ability to inspire and bring out the best in any player with her methods.

So, I mooned her.

Reasonable response for someone fighting authority at that age, right? Okay, that literally made me an ass, but it happened. It took her four years, but she got me back for it, and did she ever! Talk about a long con. Coach Le Duc got me a graduation card with little cows "moooooooning" me. I laughed with her as she relished in that well-deserved moment. Nicely done, Coach.

Dad Takes over My Curriculum

I hadn't gotten the best grades in my freshman year, like my first C ever in music theory, so Dad took away all my music classes and activities and switched me over to business and economic courses. I had nurtured dreams of being a music major, so when Dad took over the reins of my college career and planned out my next three years without music courses, I was pretty upset, but I had to go along with it. He wanted me to minor in French too, but I was able to negotiate a minor in history instead.

It wasn't until after my father died that I realized how much time and effort he had put into carefully choosing my courses and classes for me, with my success in mind, so that I wouldn't have to struggle with it. He probably did a lot of the planning during his many sleepless nights, as it turned out.

*We understand death only after it has placed its hands
on someone we love.*

—Anne L. de Stael

* 12 *
My World Upended

Excerpt from Mom's January 1999 letter to the Walkers:

Dear Lora, Jerry, and Sharon,

1998 was full of ups and downs for us, and I think now we are on a plateau. The year began with the move back to California. Obviously, we did not go back, but we had the option to return. There was no guarantee David would still have a job after two years, and most certainly I would have to find a job. Worst of all, our horses would eat up any small patch of grass we could locate in So Cal within two days and be hungry and go pester the neighbors.

All in all, we felt it economically in our favor to remain on the ranch. David still works as before, and not much has changed for him other than he has been swamped since June. Each time he thinks he sees the light at the end of the tunnel, he has been mistaken. It has been a locomotive . . .

Dana started college (can you believe it!). She attends Agnes Scott in Decatur, GA. It is a small (850) but excellent women's liberal arts college. She is one hour from home and lives on campus. It is like one giant sorority, and she loves it. It is adjacent to Emory and Georgia Tech, so she finds her way by car to the other sorts of entertainment. She can also take classes at either school if she chooses. Currently, she is majoring in music and thinks she would like to be a high school band director. But things can change.

And things did change, although my mother couldn't possibly have known just how drastically, and only a few short months later. In fact, none of us had the slightest idea of the events that had already been set in motion.

Out of Nowhere

I went home for another brief summer between my freshman and sophomore years. I felt older, more mature, and I enjoyed a new sense of independence by then. I'd been off on my own, exploring and trying new things like clubbing, sex, and drinking. I felt there was no turning back; I'd left my childhood behind me forever.

Unfortunately, this was also when I wrecked my car again. My parents didn't replace it, so I mainly stayed at home, but I served a little at the same Gainesville sports bar, lifeguarded a bit, and dated.

We were all about to leave the house one day, already at the door, just waiting for Mom. But, to our surprise, she was still sitting in the living room. We knew she'd been a little tired lately, but that was all. Dad tried to touch her shoulder, and we suddenly realized by her reaction that she was in a great deal of pain. He asked if she was okay, and she said she didn't feel well. Then, she started making odd, short little cries like she couldn't breathe and suddenly slumped over.

Dad took her to the ER while Stephen and I stayed home. It turned out Mom had pneumonia and ended up in the hospital for a few days. This had come out of nowhere, as far as we were concerned. We had no idea anything was going on with her.

What Did I Miss?

Shortly after that incident, I went back to Agnes Scott as a sophomore. I was eager to get away from my family and back to the new life I was developing in Atlanta.

We were all concerned about my mother, but there was nothing

I could do to help, and my parents were clear about wanting me to continue with my studies. That's how I missed out on a lot of what happened after that.

Like the exploratory surgery through mucous-packed lungs that revealed multiple tumorous lumps. They turned out to be an aggressive form of adenocarcinoma, cancer of the lungs. I also missed all the hospital visits and tests Mom endured.

And I missed the diagnosis.

I think if Mom had wanted me there, or if my dad hadn't been there to support her, she would have asked for my help. And they probably didn't want to burden me, or perhaps it was partly the family dynamics of not talking about difficult, personal things. I knew I was close enough to go home if needed, but I also didn't know how serious it was.

Back at school, blissfully unaware, I was doing well with my new curriculum. Well enough, in fact, to establish a new club at Agnes Scott.

Women in Business

Joanne Mocny had worked closely with my father while he was general counsel in Georgia, which is how I got to know her. She was the first woman to hold an executive leadership position within a Japanese company in the US, quite an honor.

My father spoke highly of her personally and from a work ethic, a collaborative effort and a general leadership perspective. During my sophomore year at Agnes Scott, two girlfriends from our business and economics major and I got together and decided Agnes Scott College needed a Women in Business club. So, we founded it with my dad, Joanne, and one other gentleman as our first guests on our first panel.

I immediately became obsessed with Joanne and her successes, partly because of her status and stature but also because she "tamed" my dad in my eyes. She became a lifelong friend and mentor.

Then, in the fall, I went home for the Jewish holidays.

The Diagnosis

I noticed right away that my mom wasn't wearing a bra, which was unusual, and an unmistakable atmosphere that said something was seriously up. My parents finally told me about Mom's exploratory surgery and how significant it had been. They had cut open the upper portion of her chest, under the breast, from sternum to midway behind her back, and left her filled with major stitches and staples to put everything back together. The entire area was far too sensitive to wear a bra for a long time.

Then they told me the diagnosis: my mother had six months to live.

It scared the hell out of me. Yet I also wondered what would happen if she did die. As soon as the thought crossed my mind, guilt entered and became my constant companion for many years to come. I naïvely believed I could somehow be responsible for her death. Emotions are complex and can take years to work through, even after we're ready to let those old skeletons out of our tightly guarded closets.

We didn't discuss it anymore. Stephen knew even less than I did, and my parents made me promise not to tell him the details.

Having the exploratory surgery right before the Jewish holidays was especially tough because the three of us attended High Holiday services without Mom and had to field questions from our close friends at temple. Dad, ever the lawyer, was quick to redirect all inquiries. Close friends, people with whom they had worked side by side as volunteers, naturally asked where my mom was.

Those exchanges went pretty much like this:

Friend: "Where's Debi?"
My father: "How are you?"
Friend: "But where's Debi?"
My father: "Oh, we're good. Nice to see you."
And he would walk away with us awkwardly trailing behind.

I had learned not to share our family business with any-one. But while we intensely wanted to keep everything private, rumors had already begun spreading that my mother had can-cer. Among other things, that meant my father would not be stepping into the honored role of temple president as expected so that he could take care of her.

I think my brother was mostly clueless about what was going on, and not just because no one was filling him in. Stephen was dating his first girlfriend around that time and was probably off smooching in corners as much as possible, hormones being what they are at fifteen.

Popsicles, Chemo, and Tongue Piercings

I remember thinking Mom's diagnosis sucked as I watched her lose weight, along with her hair, eyelashes, and physical strength. It didn't happen overnight, but it seemed like it since I didn't live at home anymore. It was like day and night to me. I became more empathetic and compassionate toward my mother in the begin-ning as I observed the changes in her. I tried not to be so much of a bitch, basically.

Mom was in and out of the hospital and heavily into chemo treatments in her oncologist's living room. She took me with her one time. Mom liked to eat popsicles during her treatments, maybe to fight dry mouth, and she would sit there for hours sucking on those skinny rocket-like popsicles. On this occasion, she told a joke, and I laughed out loud. Mom saw the tongue piercing I'd been hiding from my parents all year and burst out with, "I knew it!"

My dad used to tell me, "Stop mumbling! I can't understand what you're saying!" as they tried to figure out what was going on with my suddenly awkward speech. Well, she was disap-pointed, but I kept the piercing through college and then took it out when I graduated, thinking it wasn't professional and might hurt my chances of getting a job. Now I think that attitude is nonsense, and it's precisely that diversity that makes us so wonderful.

Chip

Life continued like this over the summer. I had dated a guy from Gainesville while I was home. Greg (not his real name) was a couple of years older than me, a big deal at that age. I'd had a crush on him in high school, so at first, it was like a dream come true, but the reality was very disappointing. So, I started cheating on him with my old high school boyfriend.

Ginger, our golden lab, had died a few years before, and we'd gotten Chip, a German shorthaired pointer, to replace him. Chip was lean and muscular, with beautiful chocolate brown spots on his otherwise all-white body.

After getting home one day that fall, Dad and I were shocked to find Chip lying stiff and dead at the top of the driveway. My dad said, "I'll drop you off at the house. You go entertain your mom, and I'll take care of Chip." He said he needed me to be there with him when he told her. She was on narcotics for the pain, and he warned me, "You may see a side of her you've never seen before." So that's exactly what I did.

When Dad came in and told her Chip had been hit by a car, Mom glared accusingly at me and said, "Wow, you had me fooled. Why did you do that?" That hurt, but really, I was just doing what Dad said to do. Then my mom lost it completely, and she sobbed. Deep, convulsive sobs. Dad was right. I had never seen her like that—I'd never really seen either of my parents get emotional, and we all cried with her.

Later, my mother said she thought she knew who had done it and why. Finding Chip lying at the *top* of the driveway was suspicious, but I'll never know for sure.

This was another sad ending to one of my visits home. But there were also bright spots and great times along the way.

Birthright Israel

That winter, I had the experience of a lifetime. I went on the second-ever Birthright Israel event, a free fourteen-day journey in Israel designed for Jewish young adults. Birthright Israel is a scholarship fund put together just one year earlier, in 1998, funded initially by a group of wealthy Jews, but anyone can contribute today.

The goal is for Jewish students from all over the world to visit Israel and explore community, identity, and connection to a homeland. So, all I had to do was get transportation from Georgia to New York to catch an El Al flight to Israel.

This was a life-changing opportunity to meet Jewish students from everywhere on the planet, including my Israeli peers. I heard their stories and learned how their lives in Israel differed from our lives in America.

For one thing, their military requires every Israeli citizen to enter the military for about three years. Knowing what's coming, many Israeli teens go wild with tattoos, piercings, drinking, drugs, and sex. As the time draws closer, they live their lives full-out while they can, knowing they'll soon, abruptly, enter serious adulthood with life-threatening dangers.

There were three thousand Jewish students from all over on this trip. I met Jews from Ivy League schools like Yale and Harvard, and it surprised me to discover they were just like us. They told me it was hard as hell to get into these schools, but once you're in, they're probably just like yours. I thought that was cool. There were only two Jews in Agnes Scott at the time, and I was the only one on the trip, so everyone knew me as Agnes.

We grew close to one another on our chartered buses and to many others on the trip. Each bus had an armed guard, and all the activities had been meticulously pre-planned. We did some incredible things, like a Bedouin tour through the desert, where they set up our tents to stay in overnight, some for the guys or girls, and some co-ed.

They welcomed us with a rave-style party in the desert. There were flashing lights, glow sticks and other accessories, tons of popular club and house music, and more. Picture something straight out of MTV, only out in the middle of the desert! Crazy and truly epic.

We celebrated New Year's in a kibbutz, a settlement community unique to Israel. Kibbutzim (the plural of kibbutz) began in 1910 as agricultural settlements during the early immigration of Jews to Israel. Today, many are private, and some include industrial businesses. They've developed and diversified over the decades, but they still maintain their communal roots. And they throw a hell of a party!

We did a lot of barhopping in Tel Aviv and Jerusalem. Lots of shopping too. My favorite purchase on the entire trip was a shirt for an American beer company spelled phonetically in Hebrew. I was having a fantastic time over in Israel, living my best life so far, once again unaware of what was going on back at home.

My World Upended

I had met and started dating Sam that spring. Sam had become an important part of my life, and he was supportive about everything that was going on. I came home late spring in 2000 for about two seconds before leaving for Sam's parents' home in Connecticut for the high school graduation of his little sister, Jennifer. My parents said something like, "Great, have a good time!"

As I said, I was in and out in a flash, but I remember hearing my father screaming upstairs and my mom, still sick and in pain, running up and down the stairs to attend to him. I asked Stephen about it and he said, "Yeah, they do this all the time." *What?* Stephen was very concerned, but he was in the dark once again.

This was different from my dad's usual yelling. At one point, I asked him directly, "What's going on?" It sounded like he was in pain. I remember his exact answer: "I will tell you this: this is probably just as painful, if not more so, as giving birth." I laughed because I'd heard *nothing* was that painful. His answer was curious, though, and I felt terrible for the pain he was clearly in, but I didn't know what to do about it. This was the perfect opportunity for him to tell me what was really going on, but he didn't. Not a word.

So, Sam and I left for Connecticut. His parents graciously welcomed me into their home and their hearts. I liked them a lot, and everything was going great. Jennifer's graduation was set for the following day, and we were in the kitchen baking cookies for her post-graduation party. It was mid-morning on June 14, a date I will remember for the rest of my life, with bright sunlight bursting in and bouncing off the yellow countertop where the cookies were cooling on racks.

The phone rang, and Mr. Meyer answered it. He immediately handed the receiver over to me, saying, "David Cohen is on the phone." Again, my reaction was, *What?* That was the name of our family doctor and friend, and it didn't register that he was calling me. Why would he? As I took the receiver from Mr. Meyer, it flashed through my mind that maybe it was some kind of practical joke.

But it wasn't. Dr. Cohen said, "You've got to get home *ASAP*, Dana. Your father died."

Suddenly, the world closed in, and everything went black and heavy as the floor raced up and grabbed me. The next thing I knew, someone was helping me to my feet, asking if I was okay.

Just like that, he was gone. Of course, I knew something was up, but I didn't realize how sick he was, or I would never have left him. I would never have given up the last chance I'd ever have of seeing my father again for the rest of my life.

Death never comes at the right *time, despite what mortals believe.
Death always comes like a thief.*

—Christopher Pike

* 13 *

The Bottom Drops Out

When I came to, embarrassed at the thought of disrupting Jennifer's graduation party, I remember saying, "I will not be the reason Jennifer doesn't enjoy her graduation." If you've ever acted or said something incongruent like that, you'll understand the compartmentalization, the denial that was taking place. I was more concerned about how my reaction could affect others than dealing with the news.

It ended up being an appropriately gray, overcast, misting kind of day for her outside graduation. I kept squeezing Sam's hand as we sat on the cold, damp bleachers. Sam's mother was a saint. She helped make the arrangements for the three of us to go back home that night on a red eye. I remember going to sleep and waking up early for the flight, then the sound of the engines lulling Sam and me back to sleep with our heads lolling back and forth, mouths hanging open. They stayed with Mom, Stephen, and me while I did what I had to and began putting some of the pieces together.

Pieces of the Puzzle

Once again, while I'd been away, major events had been taking place at home. This time, my father had undergone testing for symptoms of which I was again largely unaware. It came back negative, so they did exploratory surgery. He'd been in a tremendous amount of pain, which explained the screaming and anger he'd been exhibiting. Then, in an incredibly short time, just six weeks after the doctors diagnosed my father with pancreatic cancer, he died. Just like that.

I was furious with both parents for not telling me what was going on, although I could only take it out on my mother. Furious for covering it up and not letting Stephen and me help. Furious for Mom always saying, "Everything is fine!" when everything could not possibly have been further from fine. And especially furious for preventing me from being with Dad at the end. But now the three of us were trying to deal with the unthinkable from our different perspectives, and we couldn't get on the same page to support each other.

Looking back, I'm sure my parents didn't want me worrying about my father's health, knowing it would have distracted me from my upcoming finals. But as a twenty-year-old absorbed in my new life, that never occurred to me. All I could think was that they had lied to me by not telling me, while they looked at it as— well, as just not telling me. They were used to making executive decisions without involving my brother or me, as parents must often legitimately do. But from my confident, admittedly limited, perspective, I resented being treated like a child and kept out of the decision-making process.

Shiva

I called a few relatives to inform them, and then the phone tree took over, making sure everyone knew. People set up food deliveries for my brother and me so that we wouldn't worry about meals. Words aren't always necessary for comfort; sometimes just being there is enough. And, in general, Jewish people don't ask questions; they take care of you with food and prayer.

The week after my father died was a madhouse. I felt like a crazy person, one minute having to welcome my family as they arrived from all over the world for the funeral, and then leading everyone in prayer for shiva since my mother seemed to be incapable of doing anything. Shiva is a seven-day time of mourning and comforting the deceased's immediate family, a beautiful Jewish tradition. Most of the time, I wanted everyone just to leave us alone, but it was also nice seeing friends and relatives I hadn't seen in a long time. Melanie was a big help during this time with all the arrangements.

Some of my friends from Agnes Scott surprised me by coming up from North Carolina and Georgia to stay with me. I remember waking up to find them sleeping on the floor of my bedroom! They coordinated the effort to help me during this incredibly difficult time. They are still my friends, and I still feel tremendous gratitude for their generous and loving support.

No one ever told me that grief felt so like fear.

—C. S. Lewis

It was comforting having them there as I tried to wrap my head around my father's death. It wasn't supposed to happen like that. I wasn't ready! And who was I now that he was gone? I couldn't articulate it then, but a school counselor helped me dig that one out later so I could begin to explore who I was apart from my father. I felt very small, afraid, alienated, and utterly lost without him.

Evan was one of my best friends from high school, so when his family read about shiva in the obituary notice, he and his family stopped by to pay their respects. They're Mormon but wore kippot, head coverings Jewish men usually wear as a sign of respect for G-d, to show respect to us. After that, Evan checked in on me a few times.

He was, and I'm sure still is, a very bright and caring guy. Evan and I had tried dating briefly, and while we truly loved each other, we both knew it wouldn't work because of our different religious beliefs. We lost touch over the years, but I still think fondly of him.

My brother, Stephen, was a sixteen-year-old with all kinds of issues, and life as he knew it had just ended, as it had for me. He shut down, utterly at a loss about how to deal with it. I can't imagine what he was even thinking. He began pouring himself into relationships, and that winter he had sex for the first time. He had asked me for advice, and while it wasn't something I thought I should do or that he was ready for, he needed someone to advise him. So, since Mom wasn't emotionally available—and probably wouldn't have anyway—I did.

My mother was the one who had been given a year to live, yet my father had just died. I started keeping a journal that June and filled it with angry outpourings, like this:

> *Why couldn't it have been her?*

More fuel for the guilt pyre. And I just kept heaping it on.

Women's Lib Out the Door

To add to the insanity, Mom started dating three weeks after my father died. Three *weeks*! The love of her life was barely in the grave and she was already dating another man. When I asked her about it, she said he reminded her of Daddy, and she enjoyed spending time with him. I said many harsh things to her I later regretted, but I thought it was terribly disrespectful, disloyal, and utterly bewildering to this twenty-year-old who had just lost her father.

My mother had been my role model, my inspiration for women's rights, the one who'd planted female strength deep within me, and I didn't know how to process what she was doing now. She seemed to need a man to depend on. She stopped seeing him shortly after that, but I'd lost all respect for her by then.

My brother was clinging to my mom, and I felt terrible for him. At least I had Sam and could hang out with Melanie on nights when Sam was away working. I was working at Chateau Elan, and it was hard watching all the weddings. I missed my father, and it suddenly hit me that he wouldn't be there to walk me down the aisle if I were to get married. That made me sad, but then I figured Stephen would take his place.

Another excerpt from my journal:

Tonight we partied, funny enough, at Chateau Elan for Daniel Berzack's wedding. They had his rabbi and her priest do a split ceremony, and it came across to me as the battle of the clergy. As long as Dan is happy.

Michelle looked amazing! We had tanned by her parents' pool, and her skin looked great in that purple strapless dress. She was a bridesmaid and danced the night away. I envy her sometimes.

I just got drunk and tried to keep the single dudes away from Mom. She looked gorgeous, which pissed me off. This guy who works for Mel Berzack asked me how she's doing these days and if she'd consider seeing him. I sarcastically told him to just go for it.

F* me, he asked her out. AH! Hating life right now.

By August that same year, a mere three months after my father died, Mom and Robert were a thing. I felt like Mom was completely ignoring Stephen and spending all her time with this new guy who wasn't Dad. It was especially irritating, as I was the one who had encouraged him, however unintentionally, to ask her out in the first place! As my mother pointed out to me after. He didn't even go by Rob, but *Robert*. That was over the top as far as I was concerned. I couldn't wait to go back to Atlanta and school, away from all the nonsense.

Pancreatic Cancer

I learned later that there are no symptoms in the early stages of pancreatic cancer. This prevents detection and allows the cancer to spread freely to other organs until it's too late for effective treatment. In addition, it often presses on nerves near the pancreas, causing pain in the abdomen or back. And while experts still don't understand what causes pancreatic cancer, risk factors include smoking, environmental, and lifestyle factors, as with other forms of cancer.

My father was an avid cigar smoker and former pipe smoker, and he didn't take great care of his health. David Cohen — doctor, family friend, and Dad's best buddy — told me later that my dad's weight gain, blood sugar, and onset diabetes could have contributed to it. Also, his occupation as a lawyer included *mega stress* in the job description, another lifestyle factor. But of course, I didn't know any of this then, nor did it matter. What mattered was that I was suddenly fatherless.

Melanie to the Rescue Again

Mom was still dealing with her cancer and had asked my best friend, Melanie, to help with her hair when it finally grew back after the chemo and radiation treatments. It was a tremendously difficult adjustment for my mother from her previously long, soft, beautiful hair, now gray and coarse. Melanie had an adorable pixie cut that may have inspired her, and since Mel was into hair and makeup, she provided hairpins, clips, and hair gel, and the two of them played with Mom's hair for hours on the floor.

Mom continued dating her new boyfriend, who I still fiercely resented. Throughout that summer and over the next year, I continued my angry outbursts and derogatory treatment toward her. Melanie and Mom grew close to one another during this time, despite their age difference. Some of it was a maternal thing on both sides, some was a connection to the usually MIA me with my attitude, but it also became a genuine friendship.

Mom shared the awful names I was calling her and told Mel that I hated her; Mel gave me an earful about that.

One time, I exploded and called Mom out on a cheap ankle bracelet that Robert had given her, calling her "cheap trash." Before this incident, my mother had mostly quietly and patiently put up with my angry outbursts, perhaps understanding how lost and grief-stricken I was, and that anger was the only way I could express my pain. This time, however, she slapped me across the face. I knew I deserved it, but it threw me.

I didn't like the person I had become, but I also didn't like who she had become. Especially leaving Stephen alone at home all the time while I was away at college, as it seemed to me. He was dating, struggling with just about everything, and me having to advise him instead of her. It all felt wrong, and I did not have the emotional tools to handle it well.

Journaling to Dad

By August, I was finally able to journal to my dad:

I'm struggling. I have so many unanswered questions, yet you're not here to help me answer them. I've tried to put these words to paper for a few weeks now, and I keep having to stop, walk away, and then come back to this tear-stained journal. I have been seeing Dr. Lowery at school in Atlanta once a week. He's been incredible. He's soft and speaks kindly, things you never were for me.

I'd like to say that in some ways, it's better you're gone because you're not suffering anymore. But selfishly, I am not sure I can go on living not knowing what else I could have done, other than trying to fix the obvious mistakes and errors in my life so far, to have made you proud of me. You never told me, ever.

And now, hearing it all over the place from your friends and work colleagues, it's overwhelming and hurtful. I wish their words were more comforting, as everyone seems to hope they would be to me in this awful time, but none of it is. Why couldn't you just tell ME?!

There were only two times I remember you ever allowed yourself to show any vulnerability or emotion toward me: Once when I dove across a soccer goal for a save. You were shouting and clapping on your feet from the sidelines. I remember looking over at you after making the save and how proud of me you looked...

The other time was at a piano recital when I was ten and played "Canon in D" perfectly. I practiced hard for this one, even wearing the hideous floral dress from my cousin's wedding as a junior bridesmaid. When I looked up at you for approval as I finished the piece, you pointed to a single tear you'd shed. I guess that was a proud tear, but you should have told me you were proud of me at least once.

Poor Choices

I continued throwing myself into my studies and sports until the summer of 2001, coming home as little as possible to avoid Robert. While she was still doing pretty well, Mom had tried several times to see me. She would make lunch dates for us in Atlanta, but I stood her up every time because of *him*.

He was always standing between us. I focused so much of my anger on Robert and missed out on so many opportunities to spend time with my dying mother. You can't communicate when you're coming from a place of anger, but I was too deeply entrenched to see or know anything else.

Basically, I lived from season to season in sports, from soccer to basketball to softball. I was still dating Sam but cheating on him all the time with Darren, whom I had met while we were both serving at a Decatur restaurant. The affair went on for four years, two years at the end of college and two years after.

I lied to my friend Laura for years about it, and even when she caught me kissing Darren, I convinced her it was just a friendly hug. She was always on me to treat Sam better. Then one night, Laura, Sara, and I went to a comedy improv where they asked us to write a secret nobody else knew down on a piece of paper, hand it in, and then the moderator would read some of them out loud.

So, when he read, *I actually did cheat on Sam*, it was a dramatic confession, and my friends knew it too. I loved Sam but cheating on him was a way to deal with the sense of overwhelming and unbearable pain. I *needed* to feel something else, and sex fit the bill. He was probably clueless why I was treating him this way, and I was wrong in so many ways for doing it. Sam deserved better, and I'm sure he eventually found it.

As for me, self-sabotage became a way of life for many years to come.

Another Emergency Call

After finals, I moved into a temporary summer apartment on my own, with a little help from my friends for the heavy stuff. Then, early in the morning of June 14, I got a phone call from Rob. "I'm coming to pick you up. Your mother's not doing well, and you need to be here."

My mother had recently transitioned to home hospice, so I knew she wasn't doing well. Up until May of that year, Mom had used meditation to deal with her cancer. I saw the MRI pictures that showed the effect meditation seemed to have on the size of her tumors before and after her lengthy, hours-long meditation sessions. They looked smaller and less angry after, but she seemed to give up on meditating when she started spending all her time with Rob.

I get it now that he made her feel like the beautiful and sexually attractive woman she'd always been. There's also a basic human need to be touched, and I don't blame her one bit for any of it. Now. But I hated her for it then because I didn't understand. And to be fair, I believe there was another event that hastened the end for my mother.

Kugel and the Lawsuit

We had gotten another dog in 1999, Kugel, named after the Jewish baked pudding casserole, typically made with egg noodles or potatoes that can be sweet (yum) or savory (meh). Kugel replaced Chip, whom we'd lost in that car accident mentioned earlier.

Kugel was a great dog, but he wasn't well trained. And he was, well, a dog, and a male dog at that. He would run off to the neighbor's house behind us when their female dog was in heat. The owner went back and forth, the neighbor threatening to shoot Kugel, my parents telling him to keep their dog in the house, and so on, until one day Kugel got out, ran over to visit the attractive young lady again, and the neighbor shot him. Just like that.

My parents took him to court, and when my father died, Mom continued the lawsuit by herself. It took over a year, but she finally won, and it was right after that she fell apart. I think it used up a lot of her energy. She told me later she was glad it was over but also sad because it felt like the last connection to Dad was gone. It wasn't too much later that I understood exactly what she meant.

The Bottom Drops Out

Soon after the completion of the lawsuit, Robert came to Atlanta to get me just twelve months to the day after my father's passing—June 14. He picked me up and drove me home to Gainesville, a silent and awkward ride. We finally arrived and Stephen met me at the door, very upset. Although she hadn't passed yet, he was uncomfortable being alone with Mom's motionless body, so he was glad I was there.

We went upstairs and talked with a kind nurse who answered our questions and then entered Mom's bedroom. It was dimly lit by her familiar veiled side-table lamp, giving off just the one beam of light, bathing Mom in a soft, serene glow. The nurse told us to sit and talk to her because she could still hear, although she was past the point of responding.

So, we pulled up chairs and sat next to her, sharing tearful words, telling her we loved her and wished her peace and no more pain. We sat there for what felt like an eternity. Then, at some point that evening, we went downstairs to try and eat something. We weren't there long before the nurse called us back up for my mother's last breaths.

She died then—on the *exact* same day my father had died only a year earlier, but at least I was there for her last breaths. It was very peaceful. One final breath, her body trembled almost as if she was trying to sit up, a little unnerving to Stephen and me, and then, nothing. And that's all we were left with—absolutely nothing. We were orphans, a devastating new reality we tried to wrap our heads around but couldn't. We could only hold each other and cry.

Rob was also there, which I hated, but I had enough compassion to realize that he'd lost her too, so we left the room as he held her. We gave him privacy to say his good-byes and then promptly kicked him out.

*It takes strength to make your way through grief,
to grab hold of life and let it pull you forward.*

—Patti Davis

* 14 *
Keep On Keeping On

A s I remember it, the night my mother died, our beloved family dog Hershey howled, seeming to share in my grief. I recalled something my mother told me after my father died, that Hershey had howled that night, too. I knew Hershey was part of the family, but I hadn't realized just how connected he was.

There was an awful sense of déjà vu because I *had* been through this before. My bestie, Melanie, was already there, helping once again with the arrangements. But this time was different. It was a weird situation because Mom had been dating Robert secretly, and it may have made those who knew about it uncomfortable.

Also, the timing was difficult for my friends. It was between our junior and senior years, a time of internships and making graduation plans for the following year. So, only some family members and a few friends came around.

A curious incident occurred during shiva for my mom that is still a mystery to me. One of my mother's closest friends, Shelly, stopped by to pay her respects. She whispered in my ear that she didn't mean for any of this to happen. I backed away, looking at her. I didn't know what she was referring to, and it bothered me. What was I missing? I never got an answer.

Guilt

Remember that pyre I had erected for my guilt? This was when it began burning out of control. I started journaling letters to my mother in July that same year.

> *Mother,*
>
> *The guilt I feel because of how poorly I treated you before your passing consumes me. For the life of me, I can't figure out why I was so horrible to you. Thinking of the name-calling and the time you slapped me across the face for taking it too far makes me cringe. I'm not sure you'd ever hit me other than a spanking or two as a child until that slap, but I deserved it.*
>
> *I don't know what was wrong with me, and I am so sorry. And now, I can't even earn your forgiveness because you're gone. Worse, you're gone because I wished for this, my most guilty and inner secret. To write these words down kills me. But instead, I killed you. After your first diagnosis and exploratory surgery, I wished you would just die.*
>
> *You were heavy into meditation for a time, trying to fight the cancer through the power of your mind. You would spend hours at it, exhausting yourself. You showed me the before-and-after MRI photos of how angry the tumors looked before you started meditating and how much smaller and calmer they looked after. I even tried to meditate from your influence, and I began to believe you could heal yourself. That we as humans have this homeopathic power to heal ourselves with our minds.*
>
> *But then you gave up. You started spending all your time with Ron, angering me when you would leave Stephen alone while I was in college, living my own life. Maybe I should have quit school and come home to help. I don't know, but it was a quick downhill from there, and all I can seem to feel is everything negative. The guilt eats at me.*

After Dad and then Mom died, I was desperate. I thought I'd lost the chance to earn their forgiveness forever. I thought I *needed* to earn their forgiveness. As a parent myself now, I understand we love our children unconditionally. We may get mad as hell at them, but we never, ever stop loving them, and forgiveness is part of that love. I am certain that my mother forgave me for treating her so poorly before she died, but I am still working on forgiving myself.

Ignoring Your Feelings Doesn't Make Them Go Away

I was still a child in many ways. The realization that I couldn't depend on my parents, whom I thought would always be there for me, even as I craved my independence, was terrifying. Everything was up to me now.

With one more year of college left, I thought I would have to choose my curriculum. This was when I realized just how much time and effort my father had put into selecting all my college classes. I found out he'd already done it for me and was grateful. Once I understood what was involved, I wished I could take back my complaining and thank him.

I also knew nothing about banking, paying bills, or all the other adult responsibilities I suddenly had to do for myself. But I knew I had to keep going, despite feeling as if I had the weight of the world on my shoulders.

My guidance counselor, coaches, administrators, everyone who knew me, encouraged me to take time off to grieve and find some healing. But instead, I dug deep down and kept going. I never even considered backing off. My senior year was paid for, and that was that. At least, that was my thought process. But now I understand there was a deeper reason that taking a break, certainly not dropping out, didn't even enter my head until someone mentioned it.

And why would it? My father had ingrained in me how

important education was to my future. Plus, I had nearly completed my degree and was knee-deep into my internship with the EPA (Environmental Protection Agency). Knowing myself, if I'd taken a break from college, it would have been a major struggle to go back at all. Once I'm motivated, I need to keep going and complete whatever it is I've begun.

It was also helpful to have some sense of normalcy in the emotional chaos that had become my life. I found that sense in my routines at school and sports. But not dealing with my double loss, stuffing the painful emotions down, wasn't healthy, and this is when my anger started coming out in even more destructive ways.

Anger to Deflect the Pain

After my father died, I immersed myself in sports and found some relief there. The physical activity was a temporary release from the pain, the confusion, the grief. I poured all that energy into my games. When Mom died, those feelings intensified, and the anger escalated.

I started getting into trouble often, especially in basketball. I was pushing, shoving, and knocking people down on the court. I almost got kicked off the team, and I didn't care. The anger inside burned fiercely, needing an escape. My father had taught me to keep my feelings down all my life, and now they were demanding release. I wanted to scream out loud, and I actually did a few times.

When I went clubbing, I went looking for fights. Thankfully, I didn't find any, but I came close. At six feet, 190 pounds, I guess there weren't too many people who wanted to take me on. Not surprisingly, my teammates, classmates, and friends started avoiding me. I lost a good friend for the rest of my senior year, although we made up after and are still best friends today.

Stuck in a time warp of pain and guilt, I was overly sensitive, unable to understand that people would not stop their lives and focus on my needs. Life went on for others, but not for me. I also couldn't open up and share with anyone; maybe I wouldn't have been so prickly if I had.

Mom jokes were a big thing then, and they were like daggers piercing my heart, provoking me to fire back in rage. The anger also provided a sense of control, something I desperately needed. So, for a long time, I only did things with friends based on whatever involved the least emotion.

I was also getting some nasty injuries in sports, which were perversely yet intensely satisfying. The sense of loneliness and isolation that accompanies loss can seem unbearable. I needed to feel something other than emotional pain. So, I began building a hard, protective shell around myself to keep the pain out and my fragile self safely inside, which only made me feel even more lonely and alone.

My senior year was tough, despite mainly getting As during my sophomore and junior years. I was taking advanced microeconomics, which made absolutely no sense to me because it involved the wrong side of the brain. I felt like I'd been suddenly immersed in a foreign language with no clue what was going on, and I nearly failed. The school required a minimum of C in my major to graduate, and I was a D+, which meant doing a lot of extra credit work.

I was still bartending locally and started dreaming that we needed "more sweet drinks!" and waking up in a sweat. There were also dreams about derivatives, failing my classes, and not graduating. It was time to quit the job and focus on my grades. So, with the help of my friends Laura and Elaine, I got my grades back up and passed everything, graduating in 2002 from Agnes Scott College with my business and economics degree.

Graduating into the World . . . and Europe

Sam, my boyfriend in college, had tried hard to help me learn to communicate better, to express my emotions appropriately.

He was incredibly understanding and supportive of what I was going through, but, as I've said, I continued to have meaningless encounters outside of our relationship. I knew I should treat him much better, but I felt like a runaway locomotive, unable to stop doing shitty things to others. And so, inevitably, we broke up.

After graduating, I landed a job as a financial advisor, despite a lousy economy. But I couldn't pass the Series 7 tests, so I decided to get away from everything and go to Europe. Back then, it was safer for a woman to travel alone. Besides, I had already been to other countries by then, so I was pretty savvy about traveling solo.

I stayed for two years because, rather than feeling lonely and miserable, it was empowering to meet new people from all over the world on their own spiritual journey. There is nothing like relating to complete strangers to make you realize the world is much smaller than you thought. It was humbling, and I felt protected by the anonymity. As I quietly observed, learned, and lived from one day to the next, I found it spiritually invigorating. Finally, I was ready to return.

When I got back to the States, I bought a condo in Avondale Estates, a small city in the Metro Atlanta area. I got a job and learned legal recruiting, specifically intellectual property law. I also resumed spending holidays with my aunt and uncle in Toronto.

Celebrating the Jewish Holidays in Toronto

Although Dad and Aunt Roseline had a tumultuous relationship growing up, siblings tend to grow out of any childhood animosities, and they patched things up. Years later, while researching and writing this book, I found out From Aunt Roseline exactly how it came to be that my brother and I were always welcome with her and that side of my family.

Roseline came to Gainesville after my mother's diagnosis when she was originally given six months to live. I was away at school in Atlanta at the time. My mother had just been released from the hospital; my father was stressing over how to care for her and also be productive at work, deal with my brother, etc. Roseline stayed for three weeks this visit to help out. During a private conversation with my father (her brother), he expressed to her that he was worried. He also explained how close my mother and I were.

Roseline said, "Danny, I will be here to help with anything you need with your kids, any holidays—anything." My father's side of the family referred to him as "Danny"—no idea why, maybe more French? I honestly don't know, but it was his nickname that was used as his identifier, and one could always determine which side of the family they were speaking to and what country that family member was in based on if they referred to my father as David or Danny.

Everything was turned upside down when my father died before my mother. The first Rosh Hashanah (Jewish New Year) after my father had passed was spent in Toronto at the request and in the love, open arms of my father's youngest sister, Roseline, and her family. This was also the same trip Aunt Roseline "lost" her car in the airport parking deck and had to recruit my brother, Stephen, to help her locate it. She had forgotten which level she'd parked on, which is normally not a big deal for anyone. But my mother was on oxygen at the time, with significant difficulties breathing and being active, so we sat and waited for them to bring the car to us instead.

This trip also sparked the amazingly close relationship I have with Roseline's immediate family—my uncle Willie, for example, who was always more than willing to have me visit, even generously footing the plane-fair bill on occasion when I couldn't afford it, just so I wouldn't miss out on family time around these important holidays. I had my own room in their home—they called it my room—they made me feel like I belonged there and not once treated me awkwardly. It was a blessing, and still is. Their children, my cousins who are only a few years difference in age from me, have been part of this foundation of family who helped save me during difficult times. I was enamored with my cousin Stephanie from a young age—she was everything I wanted to be: long, gorgeous hair and she crimped it in the '80s which I thought was so cool, she had a guitar-playing boyfriend back then, and she was very stylish but also kind, caring, compassionate, and self-aware. When Steph got married, she honored me with asking if I'd be a bridesmaid. I humbly accepted her ask. She's always been inspiring to me, including entrepreneurial spirit as she is a business owner as well, in therapeutic yoga/health and wellness industry.

My other cousin is one of the most empathetic, thoughtful, sensitive people I know, and we have been close friends as first cousins since we were toddlers. He took me for my first legal Canadian beer at nineteen years old. We also spent a New Year's Eve together in Atlanta around 2009-ish—he asked me if I had plans pretty early out and of course, I didn't yet, so he asked if I wanted to join him in experiencing a jam band of his liking for NYE that year at a very unique venue in downtown Atlanta, which I did. One of the best NYEs in my life.

Through this family hotspot in Toronto, I was able to grow close to my father's side and develop those next-generation relationships with his cousins' children. My father and Roseline's first cousins, Yona and Shoshana, the twins, were sisters to twin brothers as well. Two sets of twins who were siblings! One of the twin sisters, Shoshana, recently passed, a tragedy in that she had been surviving cancer for many years that would come and go but reappeared for a final tour. I had become closer with her children over the years and felt the need to be with them in support of the loss of their mother and flew to Toronto when Roseline called with the sad news. Shoshana kept a picture of her daughter and me from one of those other amazing NYE tips on her corkboard, a trip to Paris where all the first cousins reconnected, living in Yona and Bernard's home together from Christmas to New Year's. Yona's kids were all there as well. I crave that kind of closeness, that next-generation bond often. But now, I'm excited to start instilling in our children how important and wonderful these long-lasting relationships are and look forward to that new generation getting close.

Funny story: My aunt Roseline is barely five feet tall, and she always loved to show me off to everyone when we visited. "See? There is height in our family!" As if having height was an impressive achievement. That still tickles me after all these years.

The whole world can become the enemy when you lose what you love.

—Kristina McMorris, *Bridge of Scarlet Leaves*

15

. . . Until You Can't Anymore

I bought my townhome in West Midtown, Atlanta, in 2008, right before the economic shock and bank failures that moved the country toward recession, and Hersh and I moved in.

Hershey

We had Hershey since he was a cute little puppy. My dad surprised us one day by bringing this little chocolate lab home with him. Hershey had velvety soft strands of hair on his ears, like a cocker spaniel, but other than that, he had short hair.

When Hershey was young, we'd put him in his dog run when we went out. It was a four-foot-high chain-link fence, but somehow, he was always waiting for us on the wrong side of it when we got back. We couldn't figure out how he was doing it. So, one day, the family—minus me—got in the car and started driving away. From my hiding place, I watched Hershey climb out and over the fence he felt was keeping us apart. Finally, we had to electrify it to keep him safely inside.

This dog was a g-dsend. Hershey could read energy, and he would come to you when you were feeling your lowest because he *knew*. He brought the family back together after we lost Ginger.

And he was entertaining. Stephen would put a dog mat down on the floor, and Hershey would sit on it. Then Chip would drag the mat with Hershey on it across the floor.

We usually had more than one dog at a time because Dad wanted a "greeting committee" like the Cohens and the Berzacks. Their greeting committees consisted of four to six dogs and looked intimidating but would just lick you to death. We only had three at the most at any time, but that was enough for us.

Sam was spending a lot of weekends with us the summer after Dad died, and we'd hang out like it was summer camp. One weekend, he had a moment with Hershey. I didn't mention it before, but Sam was a triple major at Georgia Tech before fulfilling his co-op work experience requirement, and the NSA recruited him. He was brilliant, and his grades alone kept his whole fraternity eligible. Sam looked into Hershey's eyes and said, "Who are you?" Hershey looked at him like he understood and wanted to tell him.

After Mom died, Aunt Esther and Uncle Chuck helped me get permission to let Hershey live in my off-campus apartment. Some girls already had cats and other pets in their rooms, but not officially, as it was against Agnes Scott's rules. I wanted to do it right, so I did, and Hershey became our class mascot. I was very grateful for his companionship.

But then, in 2008, Hershey was twelve and a half—up in years for a dog. He started eating far less than usual and lost so much weight I was afraid people would think I was neglecting him. Switching his food didn't help, so I got some basic lab tests done at the vet. They confirmed he had cancer, typical for labs and older dogs in general.

Hershey lasted a few more months, but eventually, his tail stopped wagging, his smile vanished, and his nose wasn't wet anymore. He was a bag of bones and didn't move around much by then. Hersh had also become incontinent and began bleeding all over the floor, just looking up at me pitifully. It broke my heart, and we both knew it was time.

I am so grateful to my friends Sara and Lisa for their loving support during this time. They came with me to the vet, and we stayed with Hershey to the end. When they injected him, his whole body panted with his last breath; then he closed his eyes, and he was gone. Just like that. It was very peaceful, and I saw his colors as his life force departed.

I was alone that evening, and this time I howled for Hershey. I finally understood what my mom meant about losing the last link to the family.

Stephen

Stephen was seventeen years old and in high school when Mom died. She'd made her older sister, my aunt Esther, executor of her estate after Dad was gone. So when they became Stephen's legal guardians, they sent him away to boarding school in the greater Chicago area for his final year, following my mother's wishes.

It turned out to be a tragic mistake because Stephen wasn't mentally or emotionally prepared for it. The trauma of losing his parents and then having to leave his home, friends, school—everything he knew—totally undid him. I don't believe he ever recovered from it.

Some of Stephen's friends and their parents begged my family to reconsider. A few even offered to let Stephen live with them in Gainesville to finish high school in a place he knew, with people who loved him. It was the kindest thing I'd ever witnessed non-Jews do for us. They loved my brother and understood what he needed. But it was important to my aunt and uncle that they carry out my mother's wishes, so off he went.

Stephen barely graduated but went on to DePaul University in Chicago. He struggled there too, but ended up following a girl to Marquette University, so his grades must have been good enough for him to transfer. They dated for a couple of years, and although I tried to develop a relationship with her, it never happened.

Marquette was good for Stephen. He used to talk about going

to law school and becoming a lawyer like Dad, but I don't think there was ever any genuine interest. Instead, he went for an engineering degree and was welcomed into an engineering fraternity, where he made some great, long-lasting friends.

My Brother, the Cheerleader

Stephen made the collegiate basketball cheerleading squad at Marquette during the last season, while NBA player Dwyane Wade was there. My friend Sara and I visited him, and he got us tickets to one of their games. That was the happiest I'd seen him in a long time. He always seemed to be smiling and was in the best shape of his life.

Stephen was built a lot like our dad at his best, broad-shouldered, boxy, thick, and muscular. He looked more like a wrestler or football player, but, like Dad, he lacked height. Unfortunately, also like Dad, when Stephen let himself go, he rapidly put on weight everywhere, but mostly in his belly.

During the fall of Stephen's junior year at Marquette, we all got together at my cousin Gerry's house in Toronto for a bar mitzvah. Gerry, his wife, Ellen, and their three kids were all there, from oldest to youngest, Samantha, Lindsay, and Mitchell.

Stephen was totally in his element, teaching us how to do some of the cheers he performed at Marquette. Gerry took a few pictures of all of us in our workout gear. We were all grinning ear to ear, having a great time. That was the last time Stephen joined us in Toronto and the last happy thing we did together as a family.

When Stephen graduated from Marquette, he wanted me to throw him a graduation party like the one I'd had, so I did. It was costly and, like mine, we held it in a very nice restaurant with a full bar. He and his friends, other recently graduated college kids, were looking for the kegs. I explained about the bar and the venue, and he just said, "Well, this sucks." He didn't get it.

How Do I Explain Stephen?

Many people thought he was acting like a trust-fund baby—spoiled, expecting handouts, not having to work for anything. But they didn't understand *why* he was that way. He was simply incapable of living a full, normal life. Stephen didn't understand the concept of money, budgeting, getting a job, or even trying. And he didn't care to learn because he *couldn't* understand.

He had learning challenges, what some call "invisible disabilities." Things like ADD, ADHD, and other limited cognitive or emotional capabilities. I'm not even sure how well his closest friends understood Stephen. I hated having to explain him to people, feeling like I was bad-mouthing my brother when I absolutely wasn't. I don't think anyone who hasn't grown up around someone with these kinds of issues can understand what it's like, or adequately and lovingly explain what is going on with them in an understandable way.

Stephen had trouble with basic life skills. For example, he might recognize that he needed a haircut but then couldn't carry out the individual steps necessary to make it happen. Stephen wasn't completely helpless, but he never finished developing past sixteen. My brother still needed extra attention and help, and he always would.

The Final Blow

Fast forward to December 2010. I was working at a new job when Uncle David, my mom's older brother in Chicago, called me. He and Aunt Pam had been checking in with Stephen regularly, either directly or through one of his friends.

A few weeks went by without contact, so the friend went to his apartment to check on him. He knocked on the door but got no answer. Finally, his concern mounting, he got the building manager to let him into the apartment, where his worst fears were confirmed.

They found Stephen lying face down on his living room floor, and it was clear he'd been dead for a while.

When I heard the news, I went catatonic for a few seconds. Then, Walter Ozark, my good friend and colleague, took the phone from me and spoke with my uncle. He took over from there, told my bosses what had happened, and became the point person for my family. Walter even hosted shiva for us.

My friends called a few family members and other friends. Monique, another Agnes Scott pal, moved in with me for two weeks. Everyone made sure I was never alone during that time of mourning. I can honestly say that it was the worst and yet the *best* experience I've ever had, experiencing my friends' love and care. I have been blessed with the most incredible group of friends anyone could ever want.

Uncle David had been in touch with the coroner and gave her my contact information to update me directly. She called and told me Stephen had been dead for about two weeks and would get back to me when she could determine the cause of death.

Two weeks later, she called again, having determined the cause through fluid she had extracted from behind his eyeball. Stephen had untreated adult-onset diabetes caused by morbid obesity, drinking, smoking, an unhealthy diet, and a sedentary lifestyle, which led to a fatal heart attack.

The news hurled me into another storm of self-sabotage and more guilt. The hard, protective shell around me grew angry quills. No more pain. I would allow no one close enough to hurt me again.

Alone

Then it hit me like a sledgehammer: my entire immediate family was gone. Over the following month, I barely existed. I know now that I had high-functioning depression. During the day, I functioned at my job and then drank myself to sleep every night to numb my feelings. I didn't know if I would ever be okay again.

I blamed myself, feeling that I should have tried harder to intervene, that we could have prevented his death. I was angry at myself and my family. I had tried to help as best I could, and Stephen tried in his way, but he had estranged himself from the family. Especially during the holidays when everyone would ask him the same questions that he would have to give the same answers to over and over because nothing much ever changed with Stephen.

Also, both sides of our family can be inappropriate in expressing their opinions on weight gains and losses. Stephen had been putting on weight, so he distanced himself to prevent the senseless, guilt-inducing "interrogations."

I questioned everything I thought I knew was true. My anger continued to pour out at anyone and everyone until even my closest friends began avoiding me. Finally, I realized I couldn't go on like that forever, drinking myself into oblivion every night, unless I wanted to end up like my brother.

That's when I called our family friend and doctor, Andy Reisman, still my friend today. We had a long, honest talk, wherein he counseled me and prescribed a mild dose of trazodone to restore my sleep cycle and even out some of my anxieties. It served its purpose, and I was off it in six months. But I was far from being healed.

Looking Back

I couldn't journal about Stephen for a long time. I still deal with the guilt surrounding his death at the tender age of twenty-six because I believe—I *know*—it could have been avoided, and it cuts into my soul. His death feels different from those of my parents. Cancer may have several causes, depending on who you listen to, but his own life choices undeniably caused Stephen's death. He could have prolonged his life by making better, healthier choices, but he didn't, and I don't know how to accept that yet.

My cousin Gerry and his wife, Ellen, gave me a few books that they thought may be helpful with Stephen and his developmental issues. Stephen and Mitchell were very close, they were similar in many ways, and I see in Mitchell what Stephen could be like today.

Gerry and Ellen helped tremendously by sharing some positive ways to interact with my brother. They also kept reassuring me I'd done everything I could, although if I'm honest, I still don't believe that. Gerry, Ellen, and Aunt Roseline tried to calm my thought process and asked me quite reasonably what else I could have done. They said that sometimes you have to call it quits once you've done all you can because it isn't up to you anymore.

Is There a Wall?

I never thought there was a limit to how much I could have tried to do with my brother. That there may be a certain point at which you simply have to back off, to realize the change you want to see isn't going to happen, at least not right then. I wanted to believe there *was* another option. That if I had only tried that next, elusive *something*, it would have worked, my brother would make healthier choices, and he would still be alive today.

Is that what unconditional love is? Never giving up, always asking what's next on the list? I don't know. I only know that I never found it, so the guilt continued to mount.

In 2009, the year before my brother died, it felt like he was trying to force his way into my life. This was terrifying because I had visited him that winter, and what I found disgusted me. There were smoking stains on his hands and teeth, and his apartment smelled like a beer hall. It was a stereotypical bachelor pad filled with old, grease-stained pizza takeout boxes, empty beer bottles, dirty dishes, and trash. He still had friends, old and new, but they had careers and full lives, while Stephen still didn't even have a job.

Now he was telling people in Milwaukee that he planned to move to Atlanta and live near me. Or maybe even *with* me. He didn't have a job, yet he expected to live in Atlanta in a $1,500 three-bedroom apartment? He had never had to deal with life's everyday responsibilities, so I knew everything would fall on me. And as for him living with me? No way.

My family agreed and told me, in no uncertain terms, not to let him move to Atlanta. "He'll ruin your life!" I agreed and told Stephen he needed to get his act together first, and then he could live nearby. Maybe I should have let him, but I was busy dealing with my own issues. I wanted to do what was right and tried to get both sides of the family to do an intervention, but they weren't very supportive. So, Stephen and I grew apart that last year, and he spiraled.

The Younger Years

I didn't notice too much about Stephen when we were growing up. I knew my mom spent more time with him than me but didn't think much about it. Besides the age difference, when we're young, I think we tend to accept the existing family dynamics as normal, and then we sort things out as we grow older and gain a new, less egocentric perspective.

Here's what my friend Katie Walker remembers about Stephen:

> *One of my favorite memories was when Stephen got a stuffed animal he named Newnew. He loved that bear, and it went everywhere with him. One day their dog, Ginger, got hold of it and buried it in the backyard. They looked for hours and then days, but they couldn't find it, so they finally gave up and bought Stephen a new bear that looked exactly the same. But he knew it wasn't his beloved bear, so he refused it. Sometime later, Ginger dug the bear up, Debi washed him, and peace was restored.*

I remember Stephen was great with sound effects when he was little. He would play with his toys and act everything out, sounds and all. Then, for a while, he was enamored with me as his older sister before we got to the sibling fighting stage. We loved the same music and exposed each other to new kinds. We rocked out to Hootie and the Blowfish when he was in grade school, and we'd practice together, Stephen with his drumsticks and me on my sax.

But as my brother got older, he grew more and more insecure as he realized he didn't fit in anywhere with his learning disabilities and other issues.

Another snapshot from Mom's letter:

> *Little Stevie is finally taller than me, although I would never admit that to him. He claims to be 5'8. He is a freshman and still struggles with math, but the school is very willing to help. We are applying for a program that will allow him extra time on the SAT exams and special help in math.*
>
> *He plays tennis year-round and hopes to enter some tournaments this summer. He has joined a Jewish youth group (AZA) in Atlanta and spends most of his weekends there. That has enabled David and me to explore the culinary delights of Atlanta frequently . . .*

Stephen was loved. But after losing Mom and Dad and being uprooted, along with his cognitive challenges, I realized that he never had a chance. My brother died at twenty-six without his life ever really beginning.

You define your own life.
Don't let other people write your script.

—Oprah Winfrey

16

Cookie-Cutter Life Isn't for Me

By now, I'd pretty much given up on ever having a normal life. I had no hope for a fulfilling marriage, kids, or the white picket fence around a happy home. Mom, Dad, Stephen—even faithful Hershey—my entire immediate family was gone. But somehow, life goes on.

Unhealthy Relationships

Even before Stephen died, I had become comfortable with uncomfortable relationships, relationships that weren't healthy for me and wouldn't go anywhere. Often, they were simply distractions, and oddly, choosing my relationships for the wrong reasons was a form of self-protection.

Take Everette, for instance. He was in the navy, and they were always shipping him out for training, so we saw each other only six times in the two years we dated. I was head-over-heels in love with him, but then he ended the relationship—via email, not surprisingly, considering the distance and how little we saw each other.

And there was Jason. Jason was a sports trainer with great contacts in the sports world. That meant we could travel around the college football circuit and to some pro-football games. But Jason was bipolar. He frequently acted like a hermit, and about every six months or so, he would break off with me, date other women, and then come back.

I had invited my good friend Monique to come to a game with us one time. Monique—everyone liked Monique. Seriously, no one *ever* disliked Monique, except for Jason. That should have tipped me off right away! But the final straw came when he called one of my friends a racial slur to his face, and I saw him for the bigot he was. After that, I was done with Jason.

After Everette, Jason, and a few others, I decided I didn't want "normal." This turned out to be a good thing a few years down the road. In the meantime, my family kept asking me, "Don't you want to get married?" I was in my late twenties by now, and I suppose it was a reasonable question.

But I would cut them off before they could even finish asking. "No! I don't!" I had convinced myself, to some degree at least, that I didn't want what I obviously couldn't have. It was easier to pretend I didn't want genuine happiness, that I wanted these crappy relationships, rather than believe others could have it all while I couldn't. Besides, other people had their shit together, so what did I expect?

"You Don't Want to Die Alone, Do You?"

Aunt Roseline wanted to understand me, but that was impossible. She had married right from her family home in France at the tender age of nineteen, and she and my uncle Willy had been together ever since. Aunt Roseline would gently ask, "You don't want to die alone, do you?" She told me it was okay not to do it the "ordinary" way. She said to just think about being old and alone. She also encouraged me to cultivate more positive, healthy, nurturing relationships.

Because of her gentle and rational approach, I finally agreed that yes, I would be open to having a relationship with a guy with kids, maybe even a non-Jew. This change of attitude, considering someone other than the type of guy I kept choosing, opened the door to a whole new life for me. A brighter and fuller life than I could have imagined back then. But it didn't happen right away.

Making a Friend

Dustin O'Quinn was the first to welcome me when I moved into my new townhome in the Liberty Park gated community. It was the summer of 2008, and he was walking his dogs, two beagles named Faith and McGraw. Hershey and those two became friendly, so we occasionally walked our dogs together. He lived five houses down on a curve, and our back decks faced each other. Dustin also kindly let me know that one of my immediate neighbors had plugged into my deck outlet, stealing power from me. I was indebted to him for that.

For several years, there was no romantic interest between us. When Hershey died, he said he was sorry, and we saw each other only occasionally after that.

We knew very little about each other, but I knew he was an engineer and had gone to the University of Georgia. That seemed weird to me because, being from Agnes Scott College in Atlanta, we dated guys from Georgia Tech. UGA was outside my scope of consideration.

I didn't even know he was in a relationship. So, when I invited him to my housewarming party, I thought he would hook up with my friend and housemate, Sara. Six years passed by in this way, with Dustin and me friendly neighbors, living our own separate lives. And I was still interested in dating.

Sometimes it takes a wrong turn to get you to the right place.

—Mandy Halel

✳ 17 ✳

The Last Blind Date

I t was another hot and humid Atlanta night one Monday in July 2013, and I already had that annoying, sweaty upper lip as I walked into a local dive bar off Huff Road in the West Midtown area. The bar is now called the Whelan, but it was Corner Tavern back then, and I was there to meet another blind date from the Jewish dating site I'd been using, a popular Jewish dating site.

I was on the dating app at the insistence of my good friend Jasmine, whom I'd met at my job. I had just broken up with Caleb after dating him for six months. Caleb was a Christian, so it didn't work out, and my friend Jasmine, looking out for me, insisted I date only Jewish men from here on out.

The problem was, I'd had so many lousy blind dates from this dating app that I didn't have high expectations anymore. But you never know, right? Prior experience taught me that this one was probably looking for his mom too, which was *not* who I wanted to be! Besides Caleb, I'd gone out with the last guy three times. He was a lovely man, but I wasn't feeling any physical attraction and felt it was only fair to end it.

Say, I Know You!

As I waited with something less than enthusiasm, I got nervous, so I found a seat at the bar and ordered a drink to calm down. As fate (?) would have it, I sat next to a cute blond guy and next to him, a handsome brown-haired guy, whom I recognized as my neighbor Dustin. Dustin and I had recently begun to talk more, especially about our career objectives. He wanted to do more with his engineering and management skills, work on a national level, and make a real difference.

He had just started a new job at another engineering firm while I—well, I'd just gotten fired. I had been working at a recruiting firm in Atlanta, doing well. Opportunities come and go, but hopefully, we are continually learning new things from each scenario. It turned out to be the beginning of a career I love and am still in today. It was her uncle's agency, and I got to know Robin (her mom) and Steven (her dad) through that job. This is where the foundation for my career was laid.

Fired? *Really?*

After being there for about three and a half years, I decided it was time to grow professionally. I wanted to learn more about the corporate side of talent acquisition and human resources, an opportunity that would only exist at another recruiting firm. When I returned from a two-hour interview for a job I did not get, by the way, they fired me. What they actually said was, "You can get your shit and go." Just another way to put it, I suppose, but it hurt. I thought they could have supported my desire to better myself.

The owner was also hurt by what he perceived as disloyalty to his company, despite bringing in the most revenue while I was there. We eventually parted on good terms, but I was out of a job regardless.

So, having gotten to know each other better, I joined Dustin and his friend at the bar with a new level of comfort and interest.

Dustin: "What are you doing in my bar?" Smooth.

"I'm here on a blind date," I said as I flirted with his friend, who turned out to be his best friend, Clay.

They ordered me a drink and Dustin talked a big game, saying he didn't think the date would go well. And he should know because "I just broke up with the woman I thought was the love of my life." Oh. He looked around then and spotted a tall, slender, strawberry blond–haired Jewish guy and said, "Ooh, I think I just saw him walk in." Dustin took my phone and put his number in it, saying he'd check on me the next day.

My blind date spotted me. We recognized each other from the online photos, and I got up to meet him. It was one of those dates where I kept my responses to, "Um-hm . . . ," "Oh really . . . ," "I see . . . ," and "Ah . . ." always seemed to be appropriate. In other words, I was bored to tears. He talked my ear off about his relationship with his mother (and you thought I was kidding) and politics that were radically different from mine. But I consoled myself with the fact that I got a free meal out of it.

At last, we got up to go, and I noticed Dustin and his friend had already left. He had been right after all. More than that, it turned out to be my last blind date.

Feels Like the First Time

True to his word, Dustin texted me the next day and asked how it went. I laughed and said, "Not well."

He came back with, "How about I take you out to make up for it?"

What did I have to lose? "Sure."

"Okay, Thursday"—two days hence—"I'll pick you up, and we'll go to Eleanor's."

Date made.

I told Jasmine, and together we tried to research what kind of place Eleanor's was, but we couldn't find it anywhere. We asked around, and it seemed no one had heard of *anything* called Eleanor's. I was confused but not too concerned. After all, it wasn't like Dustin was a complete stranger.

Jasmine, still looking out for me, knew Dustin wasn't Jewish, so she referred to him as "the neighbor." She was trying to discourage me from becoming interested in him so that I wouldn't get hurt again.

Thursday evening came, along with Dustin knocking at my door. He handed me some beautiful flowers, and I thought, *Okay, this guy is an upgrade for sure.* First date flowers—check. Drives his own vehicle—check. Has a job, a *career*—double-check. Great so far!

Then he laid it on me: "So, the battery in my truck died." I knew he had a cute, old, champagne-colored pickup truck. Still, my heart sank as my excitement dissipated and the old, familiar feeling of disappointment settled in. I'm sure it showed in my face, but I couldn't help it. I couldn't believe it was happening to me again. Dustin must have noticed, but he said, "Let's go get the battery now." He had a plan.

I drove a fun and rare, limited edition all-terrain SUV painted a black cherry pearl, a deep purple with a bright white top. So, we took my SUV, and he drove us to the auto store, got the battery, and then headed out for dinner.

My curiosity got the better of me. "So, tell me about Eleanor's. I couldn't find anything about it!"

He just smiled and said, "It's a surprise."

There's something you need to know about Dustin. I didn't know it then, but he has got to be the world's worst secret keeper. Somehow, he managed it this time, and soon we pulled up and parked in front of Muss and Turner, a well-known kosher deli and restaurant. I looked around, but there was no sign of Eleanor anything. I was utterly baffled, but he said, "Let's go," so we went.

We walked into Muss and Turner, and as we walked past the hostess, Dustin told her, "We're going to Eleanor's." She said, "Okay," looked at me, still standing in front of her wood podium, confused, and gestured for me to follow him. Dustin was already across the dining room, approaching a giant metal freezer door.

A Horror Movie Moment

For one terrible moment, I felt like I was in a scene from a horror movie, blindly following the deranged killer while the audience is shouting, "Stop! Stop, you idiot!" I watched as Dustin opened the freezer door, revealing a beautiful, wood-paneled hallway with bread racks along the sides, delicately lit with a few soft light bulbs. I'm even more confused now, but I still follow him in. Just like those movies, because now I'm thinking I'm trapped, about to be sold off in some sort of trafficking scheme, but I'm walking in anyway.

The hallway curved a bit and brought us to a dead stop in front of a pair of lush, heavy, dark black-velvet curtains that flowed to the floor. Dustin pulled them apart with his powerful arms, and as I cautiously peered in, I saw a small, intimate, dimly lit speakeasy called . . . Eleanor's. Clearly, Eleanor's was one of the best-kept secrets in Atlanta. I see Dustin high-five the manager and think to myself, *Oh, this guy is good.* I also think, *He's getting laid.*

So, we go in, sit at the bar, and Dustin orders each of us the best Reuben sandwich I've ever had. He drank bourbon, I drank scotch, and we spent the next couple of hours trying to stump each other with movie quotes. My level of movie quoting is high, and I'd not met anyone even close to my level before. He was quite good.

When I told Jasmine about it the next day, she was still doubtful, still being a great friend looking out for me. But when I went into more detail, she finally came around, saying, "Oh, honey, you need to marry that one." She understood that he "got" me, and she approved. Jasmine is still one of our closest friends.

*Clouds come floating into my life, no longer to carry rain
or usher storm, but to add color to my sunset sky.*

—Rabindranath Tagore

18
Learning to Live with Hope

T hings progressed rapidly after that amazing first date. Barely three months later, Dustin moved me into his townhome, just in time for college football season.

I felt safe enough to begin making plans for a future with him. What a relief to finally let go of the pretense that crappy relationships were okay, and second-best acceptable. Because, of course, I was only pretending. We all want to love, be loved, and be happy, whatever that means for us.

In ten months, we were engaged. But, unlike our first date, Dustin's proposal wasn't romantic. Not at all! In fact, it was more like a great business offer.

The Non-Proposal

We were already talking about building our dream home in Atlanta and figured we'd let everyone know we were engaged after we got the loan. So, one lovely spring day in April 2014, we were admiring the new back deck our friends, Tom and Nat Monroe, had recently built. We'd just spent a perfect day with them and now we were relaxing, listening to the birds chirping, enjoying drinks and smiles all around.

We were both falling in love with Brookhaven, an up-and-coming Atlanta suburb ITP (inside the perimeter). Our friends said we should start looking for a lot immediately, so we went

home and earnestly discussed what we wanted for our life together. We decided to move forward right away and buy land in
Brookhaven. After a mad rush to the bank to secure the funds
and some finagling at my job, we got it.

Dustin's non-proposal happened on a Thursday soon after se-
curing the loan. "I've been saving up to buy you a beautiful engagement ring this weekend, but we *could* put the money toward
the house instead. It's up to you."

Without skipping a beat, I answered, "Forget the ring, put a
house on it!"

I had my mother's gorgeous two-carat, princess-cut diamond
engagement ring that I'd always admired. I knew I'd be perfectly
content to wear that sparkler for a while.

A "Gotta Listen to the Signs" Moment

As I mentioned earlier, when Dustin and I were still newly dating, I was in a bit of a pickle, being unemployed.

One day Joanne Mocny, my father's friend and coworker from
their time together, and I met for lunch. We discussed the possibility of my starting as a contractor on her HR team with the potential
of it becoming a full-time, direct-hire position. Of course, I was
ecstatic about the opportunity, and they brought me on board.

In the meantime, Dustin was doing great. He'd just made the
career move of a lifetime by joining a major private-sector transportation engineering consulting firm in Atlanta. He'd also just
gotten the highest salary offer so far in his career. But one excellent salary wasn't enough to get us the total funding we needed
for the construction loan. I now faced the challenge of approaching Joanne to ask for a full-time position at a specific salary,
guaranteed for a minimum of six months.

I needn't have worried because Joanne came through again.
She prepped me for speaking with Peter, the company owner.
She reminded me that I had become his right-hand girl in the
year I'd been there, and I'd also recruited his newest local and
international team members. That meeting went well, so I set one

up between Peter, Joanne, and our mortgage lender, who became a friend during the process.

This was so above and beyond what I could have hoped for. I learned later from our mortgage lender some of the incredibly kind things both Peter and Joanne said on my behalf as they worked together to develop a plan that would give us what we needed. It was surreal. They made our loan happen by offering me a full-time position at the salary I needed so Dustin and I could build our dream home, where we live today.

I am still in touch with Joanne and Peter, and to bring the story full circle, Peter's company became our first client when I started my company, HIVE, in 2017, and Joanne is still my mentor and friend.

Planning Our Dream Home *and* Wedding

We bought the land and started building our forever home in 2014 while we planned our wedding. People wonder how we survived managing both, each being a major life event and top ten life stressor by itself. I credit my husband for that success. He worked hard to get to know me, and then helped me through the process. We spent early Saturday mornings in bed perusing home-inspiration sites for ideas for our new home; he'd ask me what I liked, what I didn't like, and why.

It turns out we both love the rustic industrial style, warm and serene colors for specific rooms, and so on. Because of Dustin's organization and determination to reduce the stress on me as much as possible, most of the actual decision-making process was relatively easy. Thus, work began on building our new home in October 2014. It took about eight months to construct, so we were already living in our new home when we got married and showed it off to our friends and families.

Fairy Tale and Reality

Sounds like a fairy tale, right? It was, yet I had constant

doubts, especially in the very beginning. I didn't feel like I deserved all the wonderful things that were suddenly happening to me, and I struggled.

Dustin was incredibly patient and helped me understand that loss is part of life, all part of the journey. I sort of understood when my grandfather died way back in elementary school and again in 2010 when I lost my brother, but we learn the hard lessons over time.

Let me tell you a little more about my husband. Dustin is kind and loving, but he is also a force to be reckoned with. He's a civil engineer by profession, but he's also a working *machine* and a perfectionist. The man can act like he's curing cancer instead of fixing Georgia infrastructure; he's that passionate about whatever he does.

I've learned that part of the enjoyment and ongoing effort necessary to make the strong partnership we were building is communication and understanding how my partner reacts to things. So, while things were nowhere near perfect, they were as close to it as I'd ever experienced.

Wedding Bells

Getting there was not a smooth process. There were conflicts with the family, and I had to stand up for myself. I was respectful but firm about the kind of wedding we wanted.

They wanted, maybe even needed, a *simcha* to enjoy, a massive celebration after everything we'd all been through. My family was looking forward to honoring Dustin and me in a big way, but I wanted a small ceremony with only our bridal party and *then* have a huge celebration party. My family, however, wanted to be at the ceremony, and most of them fought me hard on it.

I understood where they were coming from, but I didn't want a grand wedding ceremony. I was afraid of losing it big time because I was still so vulnerable. I don't cry easily, and when I do, it's in private because it's a deep release of pain. I also don't like showing weakness to others, and I knew I couldn't walk down the aisle with all those eyes on me and keep it together. And I was keenly aware that neither my father nor my brother was there to make the walk with me.

In the end, asking my family to respect my wishes was enough for them, and everything worked out. On August 21, 2015, a beautiful summer day in Atlanta, we were married. The wedding was spectacular, thanks in part to my good friend David and his events company, and to my great friend Mike, who volunteered to walk me down the aisle. He said he was honored to do it, and I gratefully accepted. I'd met Mike in college, and we remained friends over the years. I consider him a saint.

We read our wedding vows, which perfectly expressed our love and journey toward finding each other. And so we became husband and wife.

Honeymooning in Europe

We left for our honeymoon in September, and it was everything a honeymoon in Europe was supposed to be. Leisurely discussions over coffee and breakfast in bed, relaxing on terraces around Europe, and dreaming about retiring in the south of France. I had already been to Europe, but apart from the obvious sexual energy, being there with my new husband was a whole new experience. I felt like I had hit the jackpot!

The understanding that I had found a life partner kept washing over me. I recalled Aunt Roseline's loving concerns and knew I wouldn't be alone anymore. There were still moments of insecurity and doubt, but I was truly happy. I felt a deep sense of fulfillment for the first time.

No Fairytale Pregnancy

We came back in October, and I got pregnant on our first try. I had a job by then but resigned because it was such a rough pregnancy. It began with six months of hyperemesis, a more severe form of the typical morning sickness. I had persistent nausea and uncontrollable vomiting, difficulty eating, and I was exhausted but unable to sleep.

I was grateful when that finally ended. But then I went right into gestational diabetes, meaning I did not have diabetes pre-pregnancy, so I had to watch my blood sugar level.

My doctor tried a few medications, but the thing that finally worked was a ridiculously strict diet and checking my blood sugar multiple times daily. I weighed less pregnant than I did pre-pregnancy because I was pretty much only able to eat full-fat yogurt, cucumbers, and some crackers. Ice water was about all I could stomach to drink occasionally.

I also had preeclampsia, a pregnancy complication character-ized by high blood pressure and damage to one of the body's organ systems, such as the kidneys or liver. It typically comes on after twenty weeks of pregnancy in women with no prior blood pressure condition. Preeclampsia can lead to severe complica-tions, even death, for the baby and the mother.

It was a difficult and emotionally charged time for me. I felt like I was just trying to grow this tiny human inside me, but I felt judged and punished, not knowing why. Then, during one of my weekly OB appointments, my blood pressure shot up to 200 over 220, and they sent me to the hospital for an emergency C-section.

I called Dustin, who immediately left work and found his way to my room. But before he could even sit down, the doctor en-tered and announced, "Okay, we're going to have a baby today." Dustin and I looked at each other like two deer in the headlights and mouthed, *WTF?*

And so, on June 3, 2016, at 11:30 p.m., Deagan Bernard O'Quinn made his appearance into the world six weeks early. Weighing in at seven pounds, six ounces, he spent two weeks in the NICU until his lungs finished developing and he grew strong enough to be taken home. I spent one of those weeks in the hos-pital myself, recovering.

And with the birth of our son came a whole new level of joy, healing, challenges, and hope.

The deeper that sorrow carves into your being,
the more joy you can contain.

—Khalil Gibran

* 19 *

Stepping-Stones to Healing

L ife doesn't come with a manual. Healing is a process that can take a very long time, even a lifetime. There were many stepping-stones along the way for me, accompanied by the loving support of friends and family.

I know now it took everything I went through to get me to where I am today—to *who* I am today. Had I not suffered so much loss and pain, I could not hold as much compassion or joy that I now possess.

Only someone who has been through that degree of loss can understand someone else's suffering. They can say the right things and share insight into what's coming so they're not scared by it.

Old and New Traditions

After my parents were gone, I spent many Jewish holidays in Toronto with my aunt Roseline and uncle Willy. They were always so kind and thoughtful, giving me my own room and space. My aunt and I bonded over things I would normally have tried to speak with my parents about.

I also got very close with my first cousin Gerry and his family during those visits. I didn't need to do much adulting growing up, so he and his wife, Ellen, gave me that kind of advice. Much appreciated!

When we became a family of three, we stayed with them for a few years since they had more room. That's where our son almost took his first steps, and Gerry predicted he would walk within weeks. Gerry called it—Deagan walked at nine months.

My aunt and uncle recently moved just up the road from where they lived for many years to a bigger house. It also had more room outside so they could see their grandkids during the pandemic. So now we stay with them and my cousin on a rotating basis.

Thanksgiving was one of my favorite holidays growing up. But when I lost my entire family, it became a painful reminder of everyone I was missing, and I hated it. Now, with my own little family, it has once again become a joyful and fun celebration.

Our Tribute Bathroom

While building our home, I told Dustin the story about the bathroom my mother had made for us over thirty years ago back in LA. I wanted a bathroom like it as a tribute to her grand idea. Dustin was all for it, as was our general contractor, but to our dismay, there weren't enough leftover tiles. The price of new tiles had increased drastically, and our budget was tight. Once again, Dustin came through and was willing to pay the extra cash to get me some tiles to work with.

We ended up with nine muted colors, rather than my mother's wildly bright and colorful ones. These were beautiful too, though, and I fell in love with them. It felt like my mother's spirit was sharing her creativity with me, and I ran with it. I tried to create my pattern on the floor, just as my mother had, but I struggled a bit.

Fortunately, I was working for Joanne doing in-house recruiting, and the company had various kinds of engineers with whom I had developed good relationships. So I approached a couple and asked them to help me design a random-looking pattern with those nine muted colors.

Technology prevailed, and one of them designed a fantastic pattern that appeared random. I coached the tile contractor and his team through exactly what I wanted, in semi-fluent Spanish, creating my Tribute Bathroom. The rest, as they say, is history.

Painting our house buttercream was another bow to our LA family home, which was yellow before the remodel. I also planted poppies and snapdragons to teach Deagan how to make them "talk," as my mother had taught me, and we grew a strawberry patch for us all to enjoy. Doing these kinds of things recalls fond family memories and brings everything full circle for me.

Some traditions, like these, I've intentionally incorporated into my new life. Others have happened organically, like our son running and jumping into bed with us, much as I did at his age. I know it will happen less often as he gets older, but it feels very healing for now. It forms a connectedness to when I was a little girl and contributes to a sense of wholeness, a beautiful continuity.

Learning to Trust People—Including Myself

Throughout all this newfound exciting, sometimes scary, happiness, I was still *me* inside. I was learning to let go of my protective shell and trust that I was standing on solid ground, trusting in Dustin's love for me and the new joy I was experiencing. I also needed to figure out how to live this new life. Still not cookie-cutter, but *my* life, a life that is authentic to me.

That meant giving myself permission to learn who I am without my father telling me what to do or needing his approval. Without my mother, not having to be like her and letting go of guilt and regret. Without my brother, coming to terms with the terrible senselessness I felt about his death. To forgive and love myself *as I am*, faults and all. And figuring out it's okay to be *that bitch*!

Communication is still difficult for me. But I know it's necessary for the quality of life I have now with my husband and the people who are important to me. My life as a wife, mother, and advocate for others is far from perfect, but the victories are worth all the struggles I've experienced along the way.

Many things have contributed to the healing process. I went through a year of therapy each after Mom and Dad passed. Journaling has also been therapeutic. Looking back through some of my journals in preparation for this book was surprising in some ways. I had forgotten how angry I was, how many angry and lonely tears I shed back then. Now, my tears mainly express sadness for others, and I know to look behind the anger for the real cause.

More recently, I've gotten into meditation and affirmations in a big way. Centering myself, envisioning each day and week, and then speaking them and my goals into existence has proven to be highly effective in shaping my mindset, and therefore my life.

Friendships

I am blessed to have made and kept so many friends throughout my life. I cannot overstate how important friends are, and how much I value every one of mine. They have allowed me to make amends and keep our precious friendships even through my prickliest, bitchiest times. When we're hurting, it's so easy to push people away when we need them the most.

I understand now that I did what I had to at the time to survive, and I learned not to be so hard on myself. Some of the ways I handled my losses weren't healthy, but they were steps that got me where I needed to be, and I can make healthier choices now.

My good friends Jasmine, Laura, Sara, Katja, Brooke, Monique, Caryn, Jamie, and Melanie were stellar with the support they gave me over the years. They helped me understand that I didn't have to pretend crappy relationships were okay. They always cared for me and encouraged me to value myself, but it took a while to sink in. They were there for me, staying with me when my family members died or going with me when I took Hershey to be put down. They have shared my joys too, and I hope I have been there for them.

Sports. Always.

Sports have always figured prominently in my life. They've been as much a part of me as anything else, and always will be. I made the switch to professional coaching in 2011 with AAU basketball and the Atlanta City Recreational League. The Amateur Athletic Union is one of the largest nonprofit, volunteer, multi-sport event organizations in the world.

All my players were inner-city young ladies of color, and it was life-changing for us all. I was the only White female coaching an all-Black team of young ladies, so I faced racism and judgment. Everyone wanted to know why I was there since they knew I wasn't being paid. They questioned my motives and assumed I was just a rich White girl. It was offensive at first, but when the girls, their parents, and my coaching staff explained, then I understood why they felt that way. It was eye-opening.

At some point, they realized that my only purpose in being there was to help them, to share my expertise and encouragement. I loved basketball and had played it throughout college at Division III level, but I had to quit because of my injuries. However, I didn't want to let it go completely because I still loved it and knew I had something of value to offer. It was also a way for me to give back to the community. When we understood each other's perspectives, we worked together as a team—and as people.

I also coached for Mt. Vernon in basketball and soccer for two years, then basketball and softball for the Davis Academy for a year, both private schools in the greater Atlanta area. After Davis, I reevaluated working at private schools, and for several reasons, I decided not to continue coaching there.

The pandemic slowed all that down. Pre-COVID, coaching was a huge part of my life, and I look forward to getting back to it. It takes a lot of time, energy, and dedication to be an effective coach, a lot more than showing up for practices and games. Unfortunately, my job doesn't currently allow for that level of time and dedication, but I'm working on it. The love of sports is in my blood, and I found my niche coaching young girls in middle school.

One reason I became a professional sports coach for middle school girls was that so many of them get turned off and drop out of sports at a much higher rate than boys. It's a very precarious and vulnerable time with changing hormones and natural insecurities, and I want sports to be a positive and encouraging experience for them.

In the meantime, I guess it isn't surprising that I'm known as the cheerleader among my colleagues at work. HR (human resources) and DEI (diversity, equity, and inclusion) are cheerleader positions! And coaching, encouraging, and helping people is what I do best.

Seeing My Parents Through Other Eyes

I've come to a place of greater understanding as I continue to grow and heal. I know my mother loved and forgave me for how I treated her after Dad died. She will always be a beautiful, creative, and gracious woman in my mind, and Katie saw her much as I did.

Katie Walker

After we moved to Georgia, Katie and I grew extremely close. She and her husband at the time ended up moving near us for work in the North Georgia area, and she and my mom rekindled their relationship.

Katie admitted that my mother worried about my promiscuity while I was away at school in Atlanta. I knew that one just from Mom's energy, but it was good to have her perspective.

Katie has marvelous stories to tell about my mom. She admits everything I want to know and have been curious about over the years. Katie and I are ten years apart in age, which may help account for the closeness she and my mother achieved. She looked up to my mom and thought of her as beautiful, fashionable, and inspiring, as I did.

Here's what Katie had to say:

My first memory of Debi being there for me was in sixth grade. She helped me be a Valley Girl for a Halloween dance; she teased my hair, did my makeup, and helped me dress. It boosted my confidence tremendously when the other kids in my class didn't treat me well, and for one night, I was cool. Because of Debi.

Much later, in 1997, I moved with my first husband to Atlanta, Georgia, for his job, three thousand miles away. It was a monumental move and going to a city and state we had never been to before was scary. The thing that made it okay for me was that David and Debi had moved there several years earlier. I felt like I already had family there who knew and loved me.

My first husband was drinking alcoholically, and I kept the secret from everyone. Debi was battling cancer then, and I would drive up to her house as often as I could to help. It gave me something to focus on rather than what was going on at home, but sometimes it seemed she was doing more for me than I was for her.

It devastated Debi when the chemo took her hair and eyebrows. She had been a dancer with a dancer's body, and she struggled with the toll it took on her body. One day we shopped for wigs; it was hard and loving. There were so many, and she didn't feel comfortable in any. She chose one, but I don't remember that she ever wore it. When she went out, she wore a scarf and a hat that perfectly matched her outfit. She refused to wear anything uncomfortable or that made her feel less beautiful.

The biggest gift of her friendship was the night they arrested my first husband for a DUI. It terrified me when I got the call from the police telling me to pick up his truck, get bail money, and get him at the police station. I panicked, so I called Debi in tears. She comforted me and assured me we would do it together.

She called a lawyer friend for guidance. We'd heard bad things about bail bondsmen in my county, so we didn't want to go that route. She drove over, and we were off. We pooled our cash and withdrew what we could from our banks, but we were still $100 short. I burst into tears, at a loss for what to do next.

Debi looked at me and told me we were going to buy gum. What? Debi figured I could buy a pack of gum with my debit card and get the last $100 back in cash. We called this night "Katie and Debi's Wild Adventure," after Toad's Wild Ride at a theme park. I'm sure we looked pretty silly, two frightened, grown women driving around in a sports car trying to get as much cash as we could to bail my husband out of jail.

We waited three very long hours at the jailhouse. I knew Debi didn't feel well, so I encouraged her to go home and let me take a cab home. She told me we'd do it together, that she'd only go home and worry. So she stayed with me, but I knew it had already taken a lot out of her. That was the last big thing we did together.

I only saw her two more times after that because within a couple of weeks, she was bedridden, and soon after that, she passed. I was heartbroken. My friend, my big sister, was gone. She had this infectious smile and laugh, and I couldn't believe I would never see her again. It was an especially rough time for me because in the past thirteen months we had lost David, my ex's grandmother, my grandmother, and now Debi.

I was overcome with sorrow and grief losing them all. Debi's home was always filled with her light, which reflected outward to shine on others. I can't believe she has been gone *almost twenty-one years now. In my heart, it seems like just yesterday that we were on our Wild Adventure together.*

Remembering My Father

I mainly knew one side of my father, but I've come to appreciate some of his other sides. Over the years, several of his friends shared the man they knew as David with me. Like Joanne.

Joanne Mocny

When we met for lunch that day in 2013 to discuss the possibility of my working for her, Joanne chose an Indian restaurant that had been one of my dad's favorites. I loved that thoughtfulness about her.

Joanne likes to remember my dad as a wine connoisseur. While working together, they gathered for a team celebration on one occasion. It was at a fine restaurant, and my dad had arranged for the group to eat privately in the wine cellar. She said he was clearly in his element and enthralled everyone with his knowledge of wine selection.

I love that story because it's relatable and real, and how I remember him too. He loved to entertain small groups of people who shared his love of wine and cigars. Also, totally in character, he peer-pressured many people into trying new things in those areas.

Then there are my "aunts" Charlotte and Karin's recollections. Both women went to law school at UCLA with my father and earned Aunty status in our family. These are the same ladies who infamously coached my mom on how to stand up to Dad.

Aunt Charlotte

During most of my visits back home to LA over the years, I stayed with Aunt Charlotte while I was still single. She'd tell me the best stories about my dad, which was therapeutic for her too.

Aunt Charlotte sat behind my father in an entry L1 law school class in a large lecture hall. It seems the professors loved to weed out the weak students by scrolling through the enrollment sheet and randomly calling on someone to embarrass them. She said they *never* called on my dad because no one knew how to pronounce our last name, Neiger.

Not much embarrassed my dad, but he would be embarrassed for others. Like when they didn't know the answer to a question the professor asked. Aunt Charlotte said that she would watch his neck turn redder and redder from where she sat behind him as his embarrassment for the student grew. I found this hilarious because I, too, don't easily embarrass, unless it's for others. Just like Dad.

Aunt Karin

Aunt Karin was originally from LA, but I remember her best when she lived in Pittsburg and flew in to be with us for Jewish and American holidays. She was the perpetually single, brilliant woman. My fondest memories of her are in our LA home, cooking and laughing. She was a smoker, and I gave this woman hell for it. One time I switched out some of her cigs for rolled-up pieces of white paper. She would have to unroll each one to read the notes I'd written on them, things like, *Don't do it!*

Aunt Karin once told me she'd had a crush on my dad in law school until she met my mom. She couldn't help but fall in love with her and want to become friends. Aunt Karin said if she couldn't have my dad, she could at least know he was well taken care of by my mom. It was enough just to be part of the family. I really liked that about her.

Barclay Edmundson

Barclay was another UCLA law school classmate of Dad's. Barclay is incredibly brilliant, and it was only natural that they would become such good friends. He could get Dad's attention and hold his interest. Our families became close; his wife, my mother's best friend, and their daughter, Christine, and I became fast friends.

Kate, Barclay's wife (since divorced), was my mother's best friend. I'd often giggle at my mom when she'd say out loud, "I miss Kate." I'd say, "So call." My mom would always say back, "No, Kate is going to call me." And sure enough, Kate would call. Those two were connected.

Years later, Christine asked my permission to have her wedding on June 14, the anniversary date of my parents' deaths, and, of course, I gave it. She's a gem, Christine. Who else would be that thoughtful and sensitive?

Christine's destination wedding was in Philadelphia. Dustin and I were engaged, so we decided to make a long weekend out of it. Dustin was having a cocktail at the reception with Barclay, who was taking the time to get to know him because he thought of me as family. Barclay had also been devastated by my father's passing.

Dustin tells the story best, but I'll try. They were having drinks at the bar, and Dustin explained to Barclay how he loves getting to know me better through my parents' friends' stories about my family and me. So, Barclay obligingly started telling him law school stories, some funnier than others.

Then Barclay gave Dustin the greatest description he ever could of my dad. Barclay looked directly at him at one point and said, "Look, I love David. He was my best friend, but he was a fuckin' asshole." That about sums it up! And he truly meant it in the best of ways. When my friends speak of me, they express their feelings for me this way as well.

My Favorite Memories

I have some fabulous memories of my dad, but these top the list.

Summer Send-Off

Every year we had an end-of-summer beach party at Will Rogers Beach with a group of my parents' friends that we called the Wine Group. It was a legit group of friends, mostly law school buddies and spouses, like Barclay Edmundson.

We'd get together and give summer a send-off together. It was Labor Day weekend, so there was always a classic rock marathon going on. I remember one particular Rolling Stones marathon. My father's favorite Stones song was "Brown Sugar." He'd missed it that hour and was pissy, which struck me as funny.

I remember makeshift charcuterie-style snacks and wines, lots of blankets spread out on the sand, and everyone playing table squash, the paddle tennis game similar to table tennis. It was a fantastic time that I looked forward to every year.

My Father—Wrong?

My father was wrong two times in his life, and both times I was there to rub it in. Okay, two times that I knew of growing up. And for me to catch him both times was quite the coup because I'd learned that "parents are never wrong."

The first time occurred the year we moved to Georgia, and Dad, Stephen, and I were hiking in the Amicalola Falls State Park. Dad let the two dogs off their leashes to explore, confident they would listen to him, the alpha. Instead, they immediately took off like a shot, running away as fast as they could.

Dad was nearly in tears. My brother and I were laughing our asses off because even we knew not to do that! After two long and worrisome hours for my father, they finally returned, tired and happy. All my father could say was, "Don't tell your mother."

The other occasion occurred when I was in Advanced Literature, a high school senior honors class. I happened to remark to my father, "How crazy is it that the same author of *The Importance of Being Ernest* wrote *The Picture of Dorian Gray*?"

He goes, "No, Edgar Allan Poe wrote *The Picture of Dorian Gray*."

I was 100 percent sure because we were studying Oscar Wilde in class. But my dad was equally sure, so I said, "Bet me!" And he did. He bet me a new car. He looked it up, found he was wrong, and completely turned off the conversation. I ragged on him for days about it, yelling, "You don't know anything!" I thought it was hilarious because, in all the time I'd known him, he really seemed to know everything, and I'd just caught him!

And no, he never paid off on that bet, but it wasn't really about anything other than besting my dad. Besides, this was after I'd already gotten, and wrecked, my car at sixteen.

One more story.

Rachel Who?

I started snow skiing when I was three years old. We went to Big Bear because it was considered the starter area for Californians and others on the West Coast. I made friends with the food line people, and I loved everyone there. By the time I was eight or nine, I'd graduated to Mammoth Ski Mountain, and my parents would drop me off there for ski school.

That year, I decided to change my name, so I told everyone my name was Rachel, which is my middle name. I had a great time as Rachel. When my parents came to pick me up, they announced, "We're here for Dana."

They were told there was no Dana there. My mother calmly looked around, pointed at me, and said, "That one."

When they told her my name was Rachel, she simply said to me, "Come here, Rachel."

I love that story because they went with it, no big deal. It was just a West Coast thing.

Handling Loss or Trauma

When I played on ASYO rec soccer, I met a beautiful but troubled child. She cut herself, but she was very open about it, unlike some cutters. I told my parents I thought it was a cry for help, but they didn't want to get involved. I wonder if this was her way of somehow making peace with her internal struggles.

I didn't go that route. I chose other ways of dealing with my loss and trauma, mainly anger directed outward to deflect the pain. Some people turn it inward into self-destruction, like that girl. It affects everyone differently, and we do whatever we must to get through the tough times. I am learning to be gentle and forgiving with myself, knowing I did the best I could at the time.

Loss is traumatic. It can be very difficult to deal with the intense feelings that accompany grief and loss. Whatever path we choose to get through, it's a process that can take time. Some people grow out of it, and others stay in their pain. That's when it turns into a chip on their shoulder. I was fortunate to have people in my life who I could trust, who allowed me to be open and vulnerable when I was ready.

Wounds Can Heal

I love how my husband looks at it—like a scar. The event that caused the wound fades, but you still apply salve to help the scar heal. The people I care about—Dustin, Deagan, my extended family, my friends, the girls I've coached, the people I work with, and the people my company helps—they are all my healing salve.

Attitude is a choice.
Think positive thoughts daily.
Believe in yourself.

—Pat Summitt

20
Not the End

No Bullshit. This Isn't Easy.

G-d tests the strong, so I knew I was being tested when my parents died. But I hadn't yet recovered from that loss, so it was too much when Stephen died. Believing his death had been preventable seemed to take it out of G-d's hands and put the responsibility into *mine*. That was an unbearable burden. Counseling with my rabbi has helped me learn to lean into G-d to give me strength. I'm also learning that time really does provide some of the mechanisms that contribute to healing and peace.

I firmly believe that we get to choose our responses to what happens to us in life. I felt deeply lost and like I imagine an orphan must feel, with no one to turn to and the weight of the world on my shoulders. Powerless and captive within a dark, downward spiral. But looking back, I can acknowledge it was also an excuse to do anything I could to feel *something* besides the overwhelming grief and guilt. Hence the drinking and gratuitous sex.

So, for about a month, I allowed the pain of loss to consume me. Then, finally, I realized I had to continue functioning at some level, or I'd never return to anything approaching a normal life or be a contributing part of society.

There comes a time when we need to drag ourselves out of the pit, regardless of how we got there. Wallow in the grief for as long as you need to, and don't be hard on yourself for being there. But at some point, it must be too uncomfortable to stay there, and we must realize we need to try something *different*.

Just know you're not alone in whatever you're going through, and you're not the only one going through a serious trial. Also, it may help to know there is always someone worse off than you are. Taking a new perspective can help, but we must find our way there first. There are no easy answers. It takes time, and it takes help from other people.

A Slow Start to a Whirlwind Romance

Just as with my parents, my relationship with Dustin began slowly but exploded when it caught fire. Dustin insists to this day that had things not moved as quickly as they did—selling our separate homes, building our dream house together, planning our wedding, getting pregnant on the first try—none of it would have happened.

In general, I agree, but I would have preferred to have gone slower in some things. Dustin is all or nothing, whereas I like to play more in shades of gray. That said, we are both thrilled with the way things worked out!

But because everything moved so quickly, especially becoming parents barely two years from the time we started dating, there was no time to develop our relationship as a couple. We had to find a family dynamic instead. As a result, the past five years have involved a lot of challenges, struggles, victories, and growth, and we've had our share of marital therapy.

We're both learning patience as we learn how to communicate effectively in daily family and marital matters. Of course, the learning is never over, and it's also an ever-changing process. But because communication extends into everything we do and every relationship, it's worth the effort.

Challenges, Victories, and Growth

I mentioned feeling like an impostor when Dustin and I were

planning our future together, of not deserving all the good things that were suddenly mine. Five years into the marriage, I still have those moments of insecurity and instability; that's why I'm still in therapy.

There are moments when I want to cut and run, to withdraw into a place of safety. Moments when I wonder, *How did I get here?* Dustin knows how my mind works, and he knew that had we not moved at warp speed, I may never have been able to stay with it and get to where we are today.

We both have our own traumas to deal with, but I don't want to tell Dustin's story. We all have insecurities, and I only want to say that our traumas clash significantly. But, at the same time, each of us needs to be true to who we are.

One area that's still a big trigger for me is when I get yelled at. Given my father's penchant for shouting hurtful things in my face, it isn't surprising. Not so much in my job, where it happens frequently because of the sensitive areas of diversity and inclusion I work in—I can compartmentalize those outbursts and pretty much ignore them. I was, after all, basically trained not to respond. But when it happens in close relationships, especially in my marriage, it's a huge trigger and a complete turnoff. My husband is a very passionate man and, no surprise, doesn't always speak to me in the way I need him to. Years of therapy have helped enormously, but I'm still working on it. I may be working on it for the rest of my life, and that's okay.

Knowing my partner is there to support and love me is worth all the work. I'd been without that sense of love and security for so long, and I wanted to give this life a legitimate chance for success. I'm so happy I did!

New Challenges to Work Through . . . Together

One Friday morning when Deagan was three, we awoke to a badly swollen and extremely uncomfortable child. The swelling had been occurring internally for at least a month, unbeknownst to us. He woke up one morning in full-body edema and we contacted the pediatrician, who immediately sent us to CHOA, Children's Healthcare of Atlanta. We were there four days while they figured out the diagnosis and began treatment.

Deagan has nephrotic syndrome, a kidney disease that causes swelling, typically in the feet and ankles, and increases the risk of other health complications. Normally, nonpermeable cells in the kidneys become porous so that too much protein passes from the blood into the urine. Thankfully, Deagan had a relatively mild case of it.

The hardest moment for me was when I had to hold him down so they could draw blood. Someone placed Deagan in my lap and instructed me to grab his arms with both of mine in a backward hug, then put my legs over his to keep him still. I hated it, but it had to be done, so I held it together with a massive effort of will. After it was over, I had to go into the hall to release and cry for a few minutes.

I am happy to say that he seems to be doing well two years later. Because of his condition, we were concerned about getting him vaccinated at all. There weren't any definitive answers, and it didn't help that our pediatrician's office decided not to take a stance on childhood vaccines. We looked for statistics that would help guide us but didn't find many.

In the end, acting on the advice of Deagan's nephrotic specialist, we got him vaccinated, along with the COVID-19 vaccination. The specialist believed that if he got COVID without being vaccinated, it could cause major long-term issues. They didn't know what issues, but she believed they would be significantly less with the vaccine. Thank you, Dr. P, for your help and assurance during these challenging times.

Raising Deagan

As parents, I think we walk a fine line much of the time. There's a part of us that wants to parent helicopter-style, hovering, wanting to overindulge them. We want to give them all the information they need to make good choices, but we forget or don't understand that children have unique thought processes. They need to work through things in their own way and time. And they need to know they've been heard.

Thanks to my husband's leadership and coaching through everyday communication, I'm learning to listen to Deagan more and understand and support his unique thought process. I think this is why he didn't go through the Terrible Twos or Threes—whatever name experts want to give what I see as an excuse to make parents feel better about their kids' unacceptable behavior. I'm not sure it even exists! This is also why I'm not expecting everything to suddenly hit the fan when he's a teenager—because we work constantly on communication.

We're still his parents, but we try hard to understand his perspective and work within that framework. The only times we've ever had any struggle with him are when we've rushed him and not allowed him to process what he needed to in the way he needed. And, of course, we've—I've—made lots of mistakes along the way, and I know I will continue to blow it. But that deep connection between us is strong, and I firmly believe having that kind of relationship is necessary for successful parenting. It's working for us.

Here's a recent example:

I was frustrated about something and tried to speak with Dustin, but Deagan kept interrupting. Deagan got mad at me and said he was speaking first, that I interrupted him. I yelled, "Give me a f***in' minute!" His face crumpled into an expression of hurt, totally crestfallen, tears staining his eyes.

Realizing I had just wounded his spirit and severed our precious connection, I immediately went over to him, put my arms around him, and said, "I am so sorry; that was not even meant for you."

"Okay, 'cause you scared me. I didn't know why you were yelling at me." His response utterly broke me because I knew from my childhood exactly what that sense of confusion feels like. Unfortunately, I never got that conciliatory, loving hug or an apology, so being able to give Deagan what he needed in that moment was deeply satisfying.

As parents, we all have at least one thing our parents did that we swear we'll never do to our kids, right? No one is perfect, and how do you even define perfect? Even the best, most loving, and capable parents make mistakes. Being able to give Deagan love and a sense of being heard in that moment supported him and closed the gap between my unmet need and the parent I want to be for my son.

I think most parents can't *hear* in that moment; they don't understand what's going on or how key it is to reestablish the connection. We've become really good at listening to Deagan now, and it's not necessarily because I can do it on my own. My partner helps me understand Deagan and that it's all about everyday interaction and showing respect by being polite.

Deagan thought I interrupted him, so he was going to be on a one-way track about it, which is not my way. But understanding his thought process and unique anxieties, I knew I had to stop and address it right away. If I hadn't gone over to him, hugged him, and said I was sorry, he wouldn't have been able to move on.

Am I bragging about our child-raising skills? Not at all. What I want to get across is that all children are different. So why would we assume that just because we've been told something will happen, like the Terrible Twos, it will inevitably occur? Everyone has their ideas: professionals, family, friends . . . I think it's critical to remain open-minded and take the time to get to know *your* child really well. It's worth it—they're worth it.

Okay, so lest you think we're perfect parents and we agree on everything, let me assure you neither is the case. We don't agree on everything, for sure. But again, communication is key, and we're always working on that. Also, we come from different backgrounds, so we have different perspectives. This is good!

To Drive or Not to Drive . . .
Is That Even a Question Anymore?

We disagree on whether we should get Deagan a car when he turns sixteen. We do agree we will base it on where he is in life then, his grades in school, his level of emotional maturity, whether we feel he's trustworthy, etc.

To me, no sixteen-year-old should have a car. Period. After all, I wasn't necessarily a poor student or a terrible kid when my parents gave me a car at sixteen, and I wrecked it in two weeks. But that wasn't Dustin's experience, so he has a different perspective. He says that all things being equal, and we have the means to do so, yes, Deagan should get a car when he's of age. Period.

Fortunately, we have plenty of time to figure that one out! And who knows, with technological advances and other options, autonomous vehicles, and other forms of transportation, it may not even be an option by then, much less an issue. Even now, millions of young people around the world have never driven, don't need to, and have no desire to learn.

That leads me to another thought.

Where's the Resourcefulness,
the Accountability?

Stay with me here. It's a bit of a side road, but it's something I've seen over and over in my business that causes me great concern. I base my observations on the young people I've known and worked with over many years. The millennial generation, Gen Z, and Generation Alpha are all young people I adore and love collaborating with.

When I was growing up, getting my first car represented independence in a big way. For many young people today, their sense of independence seems to come from something more like, *Leave me alone.* Alone with their laptops, phones, games in a virtual reality, something that gives the *appearance* of reality. I see too many among the coming generations who are impatient and lack the accountability, innovation, and resourcefulness that could help them deal with the difficult times that eventually come to all of us.

I share all this with a sincere desire to help, point out some possible pitfalls, and encourage others along the way.

But the question here from me is this:

Will we ever need to work alone in a silo? In the spirit of remaining open-minded, should the trend flow toward less need to work well with others, then fine. I'll take this back.

And will accountability and responsibility for one's decisions and actions become a thing of the past? I don't believe so. Not, at least, in a healthy world, society, or individual life.

Too many people hide behind the anonymity social media platforms provide, thinking they can say anything and be safe. It's a huge crutch where they don't have to *communicate*. Even after reading this book, you still don't really know me. You may judge me, coming from your perspective, and that's okay. I'm just here to tell you that whatever you've been through, you can survive it. And if you don't want to get help, that's also okay. But please be open-minded.

Learning to Let Go

What we once enjoyed and deeply loved we can never lose,
for all that we love deeply becomes part of us.

—Helen Keller

I've held onto many things over the years that belonged to my parents. Everyday items, like my mother's kitchen gadgets, wine glasses, even those big wooden spoons. As they get old, crack, or break, I remind myself that they are just things. They're a tangible and comforting reminder of the past, vessels that keep me connected to the people who held and used them, but they are not the people themselves.

Still, it's hard to let go. It is a struggle in the moment, but I'm learning to make peace with the process and becoming more comfortable replacing whatever. My family is still alive in my heart, and they always will be. I am also making wonderful new memories.

I still have my grandmother's fancy lion's chair, the one my mother collapsed in from pneumonia so long ago. Over the years, we have infused it with fabulous, fresh energy from my current family, creating a delightful blend of old and new memories. These days, it sits in between our dining and living rooms, performing a significant service. At this time of year, with Atlanta's version of winter coming on, its job is to hold blankets for the three of us to cuddle up in. I can live with that, allowing the old space to store new.

Those are the physical, tangible things. The emotional elements are invisible, drawing from a vast wellspring of love, understanding, and forgiveness. Those roots are there, growing stronger every day as I move forward with intention, always learning, continually growing. I'm a work in progress.

HIVE = Giving Back

You must expect great things of yourself before you can do them.

—Michael Jordan

I feel a strong sense of responsibility and understand it is an enormous privilege, a gift, to help others in need. I believe I am uniquely qualified to help people who are suffering precisely because of everything I've been through, and people seem to sense that.

I started my company, HIVE, with my business partner and friend, Veronica, in 2017. HIVE is a talent acquisition and human resource consulting firm working mainly in the transportation engineering arena.

We named it HIVE for multiple reasons that fit together perfectly, like it was meant to *bee* (pun intended). First, both

Veronica and I have been queen bees in our lives with certain friends and family members. In fact, my Parisian cousins specifically refer to me as Queen Bee and have since we were teens. Likewise for Veronica, who has a favorite honey-based body wash. And last but certainly not least, a hive is a busy home, which we both inhabit.

Charities and Projects

We founded HIVE on specific mutual core values and principles. One of them involves local philanthropy, giving back to the town where we have been so successful. We include personal charities that are important to each member of our team.

Our first significant project, Mission Snuggle, came from an early intern who became a full-time team member and has since moved on to bigger and better things. We collected gently used stuffed animals for pets with anxieties and other pets in Atlanta-area shelters.

We're also involved with veterans, because transitioning back into society from the military can be challenging. So, HIVE made it a point to partner with a lovely veteran recruiter, former military herself, to ensure these people of service get what they need.

This includes quality employment and related individual services like résumé writing, interview preparation, dressing for success, and other help. When you've been touched by military personnel in your life, as I have, you understand how important it is to show support.

Because of my son's rare kidney disease, we got involved with Children's Healthcare of Atlanta. We wanted to do something for the sick children and their distraught, frightened parents. So, pre-pandemic, we volunteered in their first-rate arts and crafts room during the winter holiday season, helping with various winter crafts and pictures. It was great fun providing moments of distraction and opportunities for joy in the lives of both the parents and their kids, some of whom were terminal.

Veronica and I also founded a second company during the

pandemic to help provide local Black business owners with an alternative revenue stream, so they could keep their businesses going. As a person with a legal background, I am passionate about social justice and helping marginalized persons through continued education. I work at creating and spreading awareness and providing safe spaces for people because everyone deserves a safe space to be heard.

Hugs Across America?

Back in 1986, when I was a young girl, my family and I took part in the "Hands Across America" event. With anti-Semitism currently on the rise here in the US and throughout the world, plus with the isolation, fear, and everything else the pandemic brought with it, I thought a "Hugs Across America" event might be a good idea.

Any takers?

Looking Forward with Hope

Who knows what the future holds? I don't, other than that I finally *have* a future that I can look forward to. And that I do, with eager expectation and trust that whatever it holds, I can deal with it.

And I've learned a few things along the way. Like . . . things happen for a reason, and certain things need to happen for other things to happen. But that's not all; there's another dynamic involved. Once I started dealing with issues, I could take an active part in *making* things happen for myself. It's a combo: the future holds whatever you bring to it.

Fin

RESOURCES

It is never too late to be what you might have been.

—George Eliot

Note from the Author:

After losing my parents and my only sibling, I struggled for many years, lost, lonely, and intensely vulnerable. I thought no one else could possibly understand what I was going through.

I had wonderful friends and extended family members who wanted to help, but for many years, I wasn't ready to let them in. Perhaps if I had, things would have played out very differently for me.

I can't say I'm glad I lost my entire immediate family, especially the way it happened, but I can honestly say that it took everything, every side road, every dark path, to make me who I am today. Still healing but with the hope of a bright future.

This list of resources is not intended to be all-inclusive but to provide a starting point. Check locally, and if you have a trusted and safe friend, professional, family member, or a leader in your faith, talk with them.

You don't have to go it alone. Help is available, so reach out. These organizations exist to help you. And, as with everything else in life, do your due diligence and research these resources to find the right one.

*If you are having suicidal thoughts or your situation is otherwise potentially life-threatening, call Emergency Medical Services at **911** now.*

988

A new law was signed in 2020 to provide a three-digit emergency mental health crisis number, **988**, to assist people in emotional distress or suicidal crisis. Calls will be handled by highly trained National Suicide Prevention Lifeline counselors.

Scheduled to be fully operational by *July 2022*, all telephone service providers in the US are required to have the new emergency number.

Resources for Suicide Prevention

SUICIDE IS THE SECOND LEADING CAUSE OF DEATH FOR YOUNG PEOPLE BETWEEN TEN TO TWENTY-FOUR.

National Suicide Prevention Lifeline Network 24/7 Crisis Hotline

The new 988 dialing code will operate through the infrastructure of the existing National Suicide Prevention Lifeline, 1-800-273-TALK (1-800-273-8255).

Trained crisis workers are available to talk twenty-four hours a day, seven days a week. Your confidential call goes to the nearest crisis center in the Lifeline national network. These centers provide crisis counseling and mental health referrals at http://www.suicidepreventionlifeline.org/.

Crisis Text Line

Text TALK to 741-741 to text with a trained crisis counselor from the Crisis Text Line for free, 24/7.

Resources for Youth

National Alliance for Children's Grief provides resources for grieving children and teens at https://childrengrieve.org/.

Outward Bound USA is the leading provider of outdoor education programs that allow young people to explore their personal potential, currently with eleven schools nationwide. Contact them online at https://www.outwardbound.org/.

Teen Wilderness programs are Christian faith-based residential treatment programs generally used as an intervention for troubled teenagers and at-risk youth. Reach out to them online at http://teenwildernessprograms.org/youth-ranches-for-troubled-teens/.

Masters Ranch Girls Academy is for at-risk girls ages twelve to seventeen to live, learn, and heal in a safe, supportive home environment, located in Missouri. Reach out to them online at https://mastersranchgirlsacademy.org/.

Eagle Ranch is located in Flowery Branch, Georgia. Eagle Ranch provides a Christ-centered home, education, and counseling for nearly seventy boys and girls. Children are given the structure, stability, and time needed to work through a crisis situation in a program that collaborates with their families. Reach out to them online at https://eagleranch.org/.

The Jason Foundation, Inc., is an educational organization dedicated to the awareness and prevention of youth suicide. JFI believes that awareness and education are the first steps to prevention. Reach out to them online at https://jasonfoundation.com/youth-suicide/resources/.

The Dougy Center provides support, resources, and connection before and after a death. Contact them online at https://www.dougy.org/.

Resources for Veterans

Thank you for your service to our country.

24/7 Crisis Hotline: 1-800-273-8255, press 1. This is the **Suicide**

Prevention Lifeline. Chat online at https://www.veteranscrisis line.net/get-help-now/chat/ or text 838255.

Veterans Crisis Line is for veterans and their loved ones. Reach out to them online at https://www.veteranscrisisline.net. Local resources for vets: https://www.veteranscrisisline.net/get-help/local-resources. Once a veteran's telephone service provider makes **988** available, veterans can use this new option by dialing 988 and then pressing 1 to contact the Veterans Crisis Line.

Vets4Warriors provides confidential peer help to veterans, service or family members, or caregivers worldwide. Call 1-855-838-8255 or contact them online at https://www.vets4warriors.com.

Resources with a Sports Kick

Society for the Prevention of Teen Suicide has several resources, including a series of articles called "Coach Awareness: Suicide Prevention is a Team Sport." Reach out to them online at https://sptsusa.org and https://sptsusa.org/coach-awareness-series-suicide-prevention-is-a-team-sport/.

Resources for Substance Abuse

SAMHSA (Substance Abuse and Mental Health Services Administration) offers several resources for locating assistance in substance abuse and other areas. SAMHSA National Helpline twenty-four-hour referral hotline: 1-800-662-HELP (4357) or online at https://www.samhsa.gov/find-help.

Detox Local's Drug Withdrawal and Detox Guide helps find professional support for quitting drugs and alcohol. Call 866-211-0698 or online at https://www.detoxlocal.com.

Resources for Sexual Assault and Other Abuses

RAINN (Rape, Abuse, and Incest National Network Sexual

Assault Hotline): 1-800-656-HOPE (4673) or twenty-four-hour chat online at https://hotline.rainn.org/online.

National Teen Dating Abuse Helpline: Call 1-866-331-9474, text LOVEIS to 22522, or visit online at https://www.loveis respect.org.

Domestic Violence: Call 1-800-799-7233 (SAFE) for anonymous, confidential help 24/7, or online at https://ncadv.org/get-help.

Resources for ADHD, formerly known as ADD

National Alliance on Mental Illness: People with ADHD do not lack intelligence or discipline, they are simply challenged at focusing to complete tasks. For more information, support, and resources contact the NAMI HelpLine at 1-800-950-NAMI (6264), info@nami.org, or online at https://www.nami.org/About-Mental-Illness/Mental-Health-Conditions/ADHD/Support.

HelpGuide offers free mental health guidance and information at https://www.helpguide.org.

Resources for Various Disorders

Anxiety Disorders

Kidshealth offers information for teens dealing with changes in their bodies and body image, relationships, emotions, and more at https://www.kidshealth.org/en/teens/body-image.html.

Anxiety Disorders Association of America provides education and resources for anxiety disorders and depression at https://adaa.org.

S.A.F.E. Alternatives (Self-Abuse Finally Ends): Call 1-800-DONTCUT (1-800-366-8288). Dedicated to helping people end self-injurious behavior through their treatment approach, professional network, and educational resources at https://selfinjury.com.

Depression

HeadsUpGuys provides strategies for managing and preventing depression in men at http://headsupguys.org/.

Man Therapy provides resources for men's mental health issues at https://mantherapy.org.

Women are two to three times more likely than men to develop depression.

The Anxiety & Depression Society of America (ADAA) provides education and resources for women at https://adaa.org/find-help-for/women/depression.

The **National Institute of Mental Health** provides education and resources for women at https://www.nimh.nih.gov/health/publications/depression-in-women.

Eating Disorders

National Association of Anorexia Nervosa and Associated Disorders (ANAD): https://anad.org

National Eating Disorders Association: https://www.nationaleatingdisorders.org

Understanding Eating Disorders in College: https://www.bestcolleges.com/resources/eating-disorders/

Resources for Various Anonymous Discussion Groups

Adult Children of Alcoholics: http://www.adultchildren.org/

Al-Anon/Alateen: http://www.al-anon.alateen.org/

Alcoholics Anonymous: http://www.alcoholics-anonymous.org

All Addictions Anonymous:
http://www.alladdictionsanonymous.com/

Anorexics and Bulimics Anonymous: https://aba12steps.org

Bettors Anonymous: http://www.bettorsanonymous.org/

Chemically Dependent Anonymous: http://www.cdaweb.org/

Clutterers Anonymous: http://www.clutterersanonymous.net/

Cocaine Anonymous: http://www.ca.org/

Compulsive Eaters Anonymous: http://www.ceahow.org/

Co-Anon/ Cocaine Anonymous: http://www.co-anon.org/

Co-Dependents Anonymous: http://www.codependents.org/

Crystal Meth Anonymous: http://www.crystalmeth.org/

Debtors Anonymous: http://debtorsanonymous.org/

Dual Diagnosis Anonymous: http://www.ddaworldwide.org/

Dual Recovery Anonymous: http://www.draonline.org/

Eating Disorders Anonymous:
http://www.eatingdisordersanonymous.org/

Emotional Health Anonymous/Emotions Anonymous:
http://www.emotionsanonymous.org/

Families Anonymous: http://www.familiesanonymous.org/

Food Addicts Anonymous: http://foodaddictsanonymous.org/

Food Addicts in Recovery Anonymous:
http://www.foodaddicts.org/

Gamblers Anonymous: http://www.gamblersanonymous.org/

Heroin Anonymous: http://www.heroin-anonymous.org/

Hepatitis C Anonymous: http://www.hcvanonymous.com/

HIV/AIDS Anonymous: http://www.hivanonymous.com/

Kleptomaniacs and Shoplifters Anonymous:
http://www.shopliftersanonymous.com/

Love Addicts Anonymous: http://www.loveaddicts.org/

Marijuana Anonymous:
http://www.marijuana-anonymous.org/

Methadone Anonymous: http://www.methadonesupport.org/

Nar-Anon: http://nar-anon.org/

Narcotics Anonymous: http://www.na.org/

Nicotine Anonymous: http://www.nicotine-anonymous.org/

Overeaters Anonymous: http://www.oa.org/

Parents Anonymous: http://www.parentsanonymous.org/

Pills Anonymous: http://groups.msn.com/PillsAnonymous

Prescription Anonymous:
http://www.prescriptionanonymous.org/

Procrastinators Anonymous:
https://procrastinators-anonymous.org

Recoveries Anonymous: http://www.r-a.org/

Recovering Couples Anonymous:
http://www.recovering-couples.org/

Schizophrenics Anonymous: http://sanonymous.com/

Self-Mutilators Anonymous:
http://www.selfmutilatorsanonymous.org/

Sex Addicts Anonymous: http://www.sexaa.org/

Sex and Love Addicts Anonymous: http://www.slaafws.org/

Sexaholics Anonymous: http://www.sa.org

Sexual Compulsive Anonymous: http://www.sca-recovery.org/

Sexual Recovery Anonymous: http://sexualrecovery.org/

Spenders Anonymous: http://www.spenders.org/

Survivors of Incest Anonymous: http://www.siawso.org/

Trauma Anonymous: http://traumaanonymous.com

Workaholics Anonymous:
http://www.workaholics-anonymous.org/

Promise me you'll always remember:
You're braver than you believe,
and stronger than you seem,
and smarter than you think.

—A. A. Milne

ABOUT THE AUTHOR

Dana Rachel Neiger is the proud co-owner of and head cheerleader at HIVE Talent Acquisition Firm, a human resources and recruiting consulting business in the Atlanta metropolitan area. She and her company are heavily involved in charitable works as a give-back to the community.

Born and raised in Santa Monica, California, she later attended and graduated from Agnes Scott College, a private women's college in Decatur, Georgia, with a bachelor's degree in business and economics.

She currently resides in a small town just outside of Atlanta, enjoying a purposeful and rewarding life with her husband, son, and three dogs in the dream home they built together.

Lightning Source UK Ltd.
Milton Keynes UK
UKHW012056040123
414846UK00013B/179/J